THE
HEREAFTER

THE
HEREAFTER

What Jesus Said About It

R. EARL ALLEN

Fleming H. Revell Company
Old Tappan, New Jersey

Scripture quotations not otherwise identified are based on and excerpted from indicated verses of the King James Version of the Bible.

Library of Congress Cataloging in Publication Data

Allen, R Earl.
  The hereafter.

    1. Jesus Christ—Teachings. 2. Future life—
Biblical teaching. I. Title.
BS2417.F7A44   232.9'54   77-20236
ISBN 0-8007-0898-9

TO Mr. and Mrs. A. N. Lovelace
of Brownwood, Texas—
Mama Grace and Papa
by marriage

CONTENTS

PREFACE

What Jesus said about the Hereafter is an intriguing study. We are living in an age in which there has been a revival of the study of "last things" and the future life. Such an emphasis is a vital part of the New Testament.

However, it must be pointed out that the New Testament presents a picture of human life that is balanced: neither the present life nor the future life is emphasized to the devaluing of the other. The faith of the Christian should enable him to have an abundant life now, as well as the hope of eternal life with God after death. This was how Jesus approached His hearers. In our teaching and preaching today we must be careful not to present an unnatural imbalance.

When one thinks of eschatology, he is often drawn to the teachings of the Pauline Epistles and the Book of Revelation. But Jesus Himself said much about "last things." Since each person is affected by the future, it is important that we know what Jesus told us about the Hereafter.

I freely acknowledge my debt to many for their help with this book. My associates, Gordon Dutile and Randy Truell, have been of great assistance. My deep appreciation is owed to Arline Harris and Barbara Brian for seeing these pages through the journey from the pulpit to the press.

R. EARL ALLEN
FORT WORTH, 1976

1—DEATH:
The Day Death Died

Jesus said: *"Because I live, ye shall live also."*

John 14:19

In our language, words have emotional qualities. It is said that the sweetest word is *mother;* the saddest word is *sin;* the harshest word is *no;* the weakest word is *if.* God's favorite word is *come.* The inevitable word is *death.*

Our generation tries to evade facing the reality of death. The fact is, death is a natural part of physical life. The chief psychologist of the Los Angeles Veterans' Hospital said, "I urge death education because I recognize that my patients do not have an acceptance of death, nor do their families."

Reading the literature of past generations, we find that our ancestors seemed to have an abnormal preoccupation with death. The thinking of our culture has gradually changed, until death is scarcely mentioned in everyday affairs. Somehow we have the idea it is not proper to speak of death in polite company. In America today, in more homes and in more lecture groups and in more conversations, it seems far more acceptable to speak openly of sex than to speak of death.

Jesus spoke of death openly and often. Yet in facing

the death of a beloved friend, He said to the sisters of Lazarus, "He that believeth in me, though he were dead, yet shall he live . . . . Believest thou this?" (John 11:25, 26).

What is your hope for yourself and for your loved ones? What is your view of death? You may refuse to think about it, but you cannot change its reality. Death is as much a part of life as birth.

We may say many things about death, but no one can hide its harshness. It is still death to die. How we wish there were some other way! Probably God's plan was to transplant His saints from this life into the afterlife by some other means, but because of the penalty of sin in the flesh, there is no other option. The punishment for sin is, God said in Genesis 2:17, "Thou shalt surely die."

For the Christian, death does not have to be feared, but it does need to be faced.

When we have to deal with death, we do everything we possibly can to avoid or camouflage it. Now those who are bereaved, according to the *Wall Street Journal,* can buy a talking tombstone. It has sixteen models. A recording of the voice of the deceased is available, also a built-in slide projector to show the great events of that person's life. You can get in on the franchise, if you wish.

Funerals have become brighter; the riderless horse has turned from black to pastel pink. I have no problem at all with the brightness of all that is arranged to dress up death, as long as it is billed as only the reflection of a great day coming. I want the brightness to proclaim my faith, rather than just camouflage my fears.

"And methinks," as the early divines would say, "there is a lot more camouflaging of fears than there is proclamation of things."

What things should we proclaim about death? The Bible declares its reality, defines its scope, and defies its pose of mastery.

Death Declared

Death must be considered realistically. It must also be *declared*. What does the New Testament say?

Speaking of eternal death in John 8:24, Jesus said, ". . . if ye believe not that I am he, ye shall die in your sins." He also said, in Luke 13:5, "Except ye repent, ye shall all likewise perish." These blunt words from the lips of Jesus leave no room for quibbling—because He whom we worship was Master of the resurrection, also.

In Matthew 25:46, Jesus revealed the final event in the process of death: "And these shall go away into everlasting punishment: but the righteous into life eternal."

The sister of Napoleon Bonaparte made the famous statement that the two inevitable things of life are death and taxes. There are many men who do not pay taxes, however. All men, without any exception, have to die. Nothing is more final than death.

Death will, first of all, terminate all earthly plans. It will put a period on your life. "Boast not thyself of to morrow; for thou knowest not what a day may bring forth" (Proverbs 27:1).

Only Jesus can change the eventual outcome. Even then, according to the apostle Paul, "The last enemy

that shall be destroyed is death" (1 Corinthians 15:26).
It marks the end of our earthly dreams and aspirations.
Hopes, desires, achievements—all of these are gone.

We may have plans for an education; we may take
out an insurance policy so that our children have the
opportunity of going to school. But the New Testament
asks, "For what is your life? It is even a vapour, that
appeareth for a little time, and then vanisheth away"
(James 4:14).

Do we not spend much more on these earthly bodies,
that live for only a relatively short time, than we do on
things of the spirit, which are eternal? Death will terminate your earthly body, and what then? "For this
corruptible must put on incorruption, and this mortal
must put on immortality," wrote the apostle Paul.
"Then shall be brought to pass the saying that is written, Death is swallowed up in victory" (1 Corinthians
15:53, 54).

The greatest problem of death is that it will terminate
not only your earthly plans and your earthly body, but
that it will terminate your day of grace.

You may say, "But I intend to accept Christ; I do
intend to make a public profession. In intend to, but I
shall choose the day." You may—or you may not. For
God's hand writes as He wills.

The prophet of God told King Hezekiah, "Thus saith
the Lord, Set thine house in order; for thou shalt die,
and not live." Hezekiah turned his face toward the wall
and wept, praying God that his days might be
lengthened. The Bible says God answered Hezekiah,
and fifteen years were added to the king's life. (*See*
2 Kings 20:1–6.)

But we never know how many days we have left. You may never again hear the voice of Jesus calling you. Never again will the Holy Spirit make His appeal to your heart. Never again will you have the option to do what you know is noble and right. Never again, because the Bible says, ". . . there is a great gulf fixed" (Luke 16:26). When a man dies unsaved, he is alienated from God.

The greatest thing about heaven will be what Jesus promised: "I go to prepare a place for you . . . . that where I am, there ye may be also" (John 14:2, 3). But the person who does not know God will not be with God. That is the second death—the reality of hell. You could spend ten thousand years in purgatory, if there were one, but you would never have the opportunity to be with God in heaven. For between the saved and the unsaved there is that great gulf, fixed by man's choice, not God's.

As Joshua said, "Choose you this day whom ye will serve" (Joshua 24:15). We all have to choose our priorities. We cannot escape death, we can only postpone it. No man can grow old without the awareness of death at his shoulder. At the age of eighty-nine, Michelangelo said, "I have reached the twenty-fourth hour of my day, and no project arises in my brain which hath not the figure of death graven over it."

Death Defined

Not all death is simply physical separation. The kind of death we mean must be *defined*. There are different kinds of death, but all are fatal.

First of all, there is spiritual death. When Adam and Eve chose to do the thing God had forbidden, they defied God. At that moment, they died spiritually.

Spiritual death is as real in God's sight, and should be as real to us, as physical death. We know what it is to mourn the death of our loved ones, but do we know what it is to have compassion over our living loved ones who are dead spiritually? Adam died spiritually when he sinned against God. He followed Satan's suggestion rather than God's will and thus became separated from God. But physical death didn't come to Adam until more than 900 years later.

Nothing will as surely cause a man to die spiritually as clinging to the material things he possesses. He smothers himself with them every time he puts them first. "For what shall it profit a man," Jesus asked, "if he shall gain the whole world, and lose his own soul?" (Mark 8:36).

One ancient philosophy had as its central thought an idea that in this atomic age modern man finds greatly alluring: "Eat, drink, and be merry, for tomorrow we die." Or, in gross language, the motto these philosophers gave birth to was "Food for the belly, and the belly for food." That was the ignoble concept of life some held.

Now we have put music to it; we have refined it and made it a little nicer with a catchy tune: "You only go round once in life, so you'd better grab all the gusto you can get!"

What kind are you getting? Or, more significantly, how long is it going to last? Gusto is here today and gone tomorrow. Only the things of the soul are permanent.

The Bible also speaks of a death so definite and final that it is called the second death. It is mentioned in Revelation 21:8: "But the fearful, and unbelieving . . . shall have their part in the lake which burneth with fire and brimstone: which is the second death."

Jesus told us to "Fear not them which kill the body . . . but rather fear him which is able to destroy both soul and body in hell" (Matthew 10:28).

Job asked the age-old question that all men yearn to have answered: "If a man die, shall he live again?" (Job 14:14). Our obvious conclusion is that Jesus' real answer to that question was: "He that believeth in me, though he were dead, yet shall he live" (John 11:25).

Death Defied

Yes, there is hope, even in death. It is death to die, but in John 5:24 we find *death defied:* "He that heareth my word, and believeth on him that sent me, hath everlasting life, and shall not come into condemnation; but is passed from death unto life." Dr. W. A. Criswell has said, "I wish to be buried with my New Testament on my chest and my index finger pointing to this verse."

"Verily, verily, I say unto you," Jesus declared, "If a man keep my saying, he shall never see death" (John 8:51). The Great Physician looked at the different kinds of death and He prescribed for each of them. For spiritual death, He provided abundant life. For physical death, He declared a coming resurrection, and for the second death, He offered eternal life in the presence of God.

On the cross, Jesus was surrounded by death; men

were dying beside Him, and His own physical death was only hours away. Yet He defied death: "It is finished!" He shouted. But who would have believed it then? Soon He gave up His spirit and some loyal followers placed His body in a tomb. He didn't defy death just on the resurrection morning; He defied death from the cross for every morning of our lives.

Have you ever been wounded by something that lodged in your flesh and had to be pulled out? The pain hurt, but then it quit hurting. On Calvary's tree, Jesus challenged spiritual death and He removed the terror and power of physical death.

A group of soldiers was sitting in a foxhole. Hand grenades were exploding here and there. One came close, and the men scattered. One sergeant, who had often experienced the presence of death, reacted just like the rest of them. Then he looked around, "You guys can come on back," he called out, "it's been defused."

"Because I live, ye shall live also," Jesus declared (John 14:19).

Now we can say to the Christian, "Have no fear, death has been defused; God has taken the penalty for us. Satan is no longer in control." Gone is the gloom of the tomb. We can fix our eyes on the glory over there in heaven with God.

"O death, where is thy sting? O grave, where is thy victory?" Paul challenged from the mountaintop of assurance God gave him. "The sting of death is sin; and the strength of sin is the law. But thanks be to God, which giveth us the victory" (1 Corinthians 15:55–57). God has defied death from Calvary, and it is defeated.

Jesus Christ burst forth from the grave in victory, and

death need never again imprison mankind. The Risen Christ has defied death on behalf of every man. "I am he that liveth, and was dead; and, behold, I am alive for evermore, Amen; and have the keys of hell and of death" (Revelation 1:18).

After Jesus' resurrection, the angels told His disciples He would come back in the same body: "This same Jesus, which is taken up from you into heaven, shall so come in like manner as ye have seen him go into heaven" (Acts 1:11). I don't believe God will leave one bone of His people in the grave for the devil to gloat over. The grave opened and everything was removed. God leaves nothing to the power of Satan; everything is resurrected.

Do I really believe in a resurrection body? Yes, indeed! But we have to face death, this great unconquerable enemy, unless Jesus comes for us before we die. He can raise us up in triumph, either way.

Peter Marshall, that great Washington preacher, as he was being put into an ambulance, said to his wife, "I'll see you in the morning." What time of day is it to the Christian? Always, it is approaching morning. Although separated here, we will meet our saved loved ones in God's eternal morning.

Christ paid the price and brought about the death of DEATH. He demonstrated that not only was He able to rise in His own body, but He was able to call others back to life.

In a play called *Lazarus Laughed,* Eugene O'Neill has pictured Lazarus standing before a cruel emperor of Rome who threatened him with death. Lazarus laughed softly, ". . . like a man in love with God," and answered, "Death is dead, Caligula. Death is dead!"

2—RESURRECTION:
You Can Live Forever

Jesus said: *"I am the resurrection, and the life."*

John 11:25

Have you ever had a little child crawl up on your lap to complain about a missing baby tooth? The tooth-fairy diversion satisfies him for a little while, but that hole begins to feel like the Grand Canyon. He asks plaintively, "Will I ever have another tooth?"

In good faith, you promise that in the not-so-distant future a more mature tooth will take that space.

Likewise, our heavenly Father promises that a more mature, celestial body will take the place of the imperfect dwelling we live in at present. We tend to make entirely too much of a physical tabernacle and not enough of the spirit of the person who dwells in that body. The person himself never dies.

God's Word does not promise merely a prolonged life, an extension of this physical life. Our bodies wear out and tend to become burdensome with age. But God promises an abundant and eternal life: the abundant life for this earth and an eternal life in a better house when the spirit leaves this body.

How can we be sure? By what we read in the Bible—that is the only source, the only hope, the only message we have. It is what God has to say to us.

Any history lover knows that the cemetery is a place of history. There is a certain pull to visit the graves of the great and the near great, the famous and the infamous. But you find that you are drawn to these places because of *who* is buried there.

In our Christian faith, however, we gather together at the tomb not because of who is buried there, but because *He is not there*. He is living, He is risen, He is not there. This is the demonstrated promise of Almighty God. The basis of our faith is the resurrection of Jesus. Belief in the resurrection undergirds our faith.

His friends and followers didn't build Jesus a monument. He never had a tomb of His own. It was a borrowed tomb that belonged to Joseph of Arimathea. Jesus didn't stay there long enough for anyone to chisel out an epitaph. The one He had was that voiced by the angels: "Why seek ye the living among the dead?" (Luke 24:5).

Herschel Hobbs has said that there are three types of witnesses to the resurrection. There is the voice of skepticism which says, "He can't rise!" There is the voice of doubt which says, "He did not rise!" Then there is that voice of truth that is evident in the hearts of those who believe that "He is risen, indeed!"

Our faith affirms the words of Jesus: "And this is the Father's will which hath sent me, that of all which he hath given me I should lose nothing, but should raise it up again at the last day" (John 6:39).

He gave us a foretaste in the example of Lazarus. The older sister, Martha, had a question about her dead brother. Many of us ask this kind of question about a hope, about a dream, about an act of life for our loved one. "Lord, if thou hadst been here, my brother had not died," she complained (John 11:21).

Jesus said to Martha, "I am the resurrection, and the life: he that believeth in me, though he were dead, yet shall he live: And whosoever liveth and believeth in me shall never die. Believest thou this?" (John 11:25, 26). This means that we shall live after we meet that last enemy, which we call death. Jesus Christ is the source of the resurrection.

The Word says Jesus laid down His life; it was voluntary, a transaction initiated by Him. ". . . I lay down my life, that I might take it again. No man taketh it from me, but I lay it down of myself. I have power to lay it down, and I have power to take it again" (John 10:17, 18). The greatest assurance of my resurrection and yours is Jesus' resurrection. In fact, that is the only proof we have, but it is enough.

Do you really believe you can live forever? How can you? Because Jesus has "become the firstfruits of them that slept" (1 Corinthians 15:20). And He said, ". . . because I live, ye shall live also" (John 14:19).

Three important facts we need to learn about the resurrection are its source, its security, and its status.

Source of the Resurrection

In each generation, the question is asked anew: "How do we know?" What is the *source of the resurrection?* What is the basis for our hope of eternal life?

Most men in the world agree that there is some form of life after death. Few religions fail to include such an assumption, some such theory, some sort of belief in a hereafter. But Christianity is unique in the fact that it doesn't proclaim just immortality, but resurrection. There is a vast difference, for the word *resurrection* means "to be bodily raised up." Christian doctrine teaches that all men shall live on, but the believer will live in a glorious resurrected body in the presence of God.

The resurrected body will be one that is designed and fashioned by our Creator. He shaped this physical body and breathed into it the living soul. So then is God able to take the remains and breathe into them and shape a celestial body, an eternal body, a resurrected body.

A dead God may be all right for those who do not believe in the resurrection. If you believe that death ends all, then a God that doesn't speak, that doesn't live, that doesn't answer prayer is all right for you—if you don't believe in life beyond the grave.

But if you believe in life after death, you have got to believe in a God that controls life and death. "God is not the God of the dead, but of the living," Jesus said (Matthew 22:32). He was conveying the truth that the believer is living and is with Him. Now He is also God of our loved ones who have finished their trip across the great stage of life.

Jesus stood by the tomb of Lazarus and called, "Lazarus, come forth!" And Lazarus, still in his grave bindings, came forth. "Loose him, and let him go," Jesus commanded. (*See* John 11:43, 44.)

When Jesus spoke the name of Lazarus, He restricted the resurrection that day to only one man. Had He said simply, "Come forth," every grave from the beginning of time would have opened to Him. He can open any grave at any time, in His own choosing.

Jesus' disciples, with shock and sorrow, had watched Him die on Calvary, then they rapidly dispersed in great fear. Yet over the next fifty days, they began to gather into small groups and to witness boldly. What made the difference? The only thing that could have changed their despair was belief in the resurrection of Jesus Christ. For if they had not believed, they would have continued to say in disappointment, like the Emmaus disciples, "We had hoped!"

Their hope was no longer in the past tense; the hope that had died in the tomb had come alive in the garden of resurrection. They believed it with all their hearts and they lived it with all their lives.

For New Testament believers, Jesus has always been the source of power as well as the source of resurrection. "I am he that liveth, and was dead," Jesus Christ declared to the apostle John on Patmos. ". . . and, behold, I am alive for evermore, Amen; and have the keys of hell and of death" (Revelation 1:18).

Security of the Resurrection

Jesus is not only the source, He is the *security of the resurrection.* We have the Word of the Lord God Omnipotent and also His demonstration: "For as Jonas was a sign unto the Ninevites, so shall also the Son of man be to this generation" (Luke 11:30).

Everyone wants to roll back the clock. In the sixteenth century a Spanish explorer, Ponce de León, came to the shores of the New World, searching for the fountain of youth. It is what we all are looking for. We seek it in every clinic, in every hospital, in every beauty shop, even in the clothes we wear. Men grab for anything that promises an extension of life. Even some on the verge of clinical death ask that their bodies be frozen, hoping that in the future a miraculous drug might restore them to vigorous health.

When Joseph Stalin lay dying, Russian scientists rushed to announce that they had developed a medicine which could enable their leader to live the 150 years for which he had expressed a desire. What a breakthrough that would have been! But the announcement was premature—the expected result has not even yet been demonstrated.

Do we look only to science for extension of life? When we gather for worship, we do not simply review some great ethic or aspect of history. Perhaps to some the resurrection is merely something we talk about in the past, but to the devoted follower of Christ it is very dear, very real, and very present; a confident part of our future. The security of our resurrection makes a difference.

In 1 Corinthians 15 the apostle Paul brought up the question, ". . . how say some among you that there is no resurrection of the dead?" (v. 12). In other words, "Where is your hope, where is your security?"

Then Paul mentioned in this chapter five things that would be our plight if Christ had not risen from the dead. First, Christ would still be dead: "But if there be no resurrection of the dead, then is Christ not risen" (v. 13).

In verse 14, Paul added, "And if Christ be not risen, then is our preaching vain . . . ." Today the world seems to think that preaching is vain. I don't believe that, or I wouldn't give my life to it. Paul said that it is beyond reason that a man should spend his life in "the foolishness of preaching" (1 Corinthians 1:21). Every word that has been preached and taught, moral and good and helpful though it may be, if Christ has not risen from the grave, the preaching and teaching is in vain.

Paul added a corollary to verse 14, ". . . and your faith is also vain." Whatever you call your experience with God, whatever you anticipate in your future, your faith is vain if Christ has not risen.

Then Paul amplified that with another thing—one that I thank God is not true: "And if Christ be not raised, your faith is vain; ye are yet in your sins" (v. 17). The cross was a mistake, then, and your sins are not forgiven. It is not a meaningful experience at all. If Christ did not rise, then you are dead in your sins and have never been forgiven anything.

If Christ was not raised, Paul said, "Then they also which are fallen asleep in Christ are perished" (v. 18). There is no hope, no security, no reality of faith. Our loved ones are forever dead, if Christ be not raised. Paul summed it all up in the next verse, one of the most poignant in the Bible: "If in this life only we have hope in Christ, we are of all men most miserable."

I believe that Christ was raised from the grave. We have security of hope because Christ is alive and He will keep His promises.

When D. L. Moody was a little boy, he lived in a small village and could hear the church bells ring each

Sunday. But during the week, the bell was not rung except when someone died. "I hated to hear that bell ring," he reminisced. "It scared me—the hopelessness of it, the toll of it. It seemed to spell out death itself." When the bell tolls for the dead, if you believe that Christ is risen from the dead, you hear overtones of joy and consolation.

David Livingstone, after thirty years as a missionary, returned from Africa to England. Standing before students at Glasgow University, he looked tall and thin and gaunt. His arm, maimed by a savage lion, hung limp at his side. "Some of you young men have asked me," he said, "if I wasted my life, and if I ever gave up hope.

"Of course I didn't give up hope!" he declared. "I went out there to that lost continent with the Lord's promise ringing in my ears: 'Lo, I am with you alway, even unto the end of the world' [Matthew 28:20]. And I came back from there knowing that He was with me whether I was there or here. Don't ever lose hope, for our God is a God of hope."

If you do not possess the hope of resurrection, you may challenge me, "Explain about the funeral you are going to conduct tomorrow!" The trip to the cemetery doesn't change the fact of resurrection. It is still true that you can live forever. To be absent from the body is no disadvantage to the Christian. Paul asserted, "We are confident, I say, and willing rather to be absent from the body, and to be present with the Lord" (2 Corinthians 5:8). Death is just separation from those of us who are left. At any age, young or old, for the Christian, death means a promotion, not a pity.

Status of the Resurrection

When we go to be with the Lord, when we follow Him in resurrection, what will our eternal life be like? What will be the *status of the resurrection?*

The Bible has several things to say about resurrection. First, our new body will be "fashioned like unto his glorious body," we read in Philippians 3:21. ". . . the dead shall be raised incorruptible, and we shall be changed," the apostle Paul declared. "For this corruptible must put on incorruption, and this mortal must put on immortality" (1 Corinthians 15:52, 53).

In our new life we will have different relationships. To the Pharisees who were baiting Him, Jesus pointed out, "Ye do err, not knowing the scriptures, nor the power of God. For in the resurrection they neither marry, nor are given in marriage, but are as the angels of God in heaven" (Matthew 22:29, 30).

Scientists say that nothing really dies; it simply changes form. Any life of animal nature, vegetable nature, or human nature never really dies. It simply changes its material form and usefulness. Everyone will be resurrected, but there will be two classes, the *just* and the *unjust*. The difference in their fate will be determined by what each one does about Christ, how you feel about His resurrection and what you do about it in your day of grace.

The attitude of the materialist is "Dust to dust, ashes to ashes"—and nothing more.

Napoleon, the cynic, had something to say: "Knock me on the head, and where is my soul?" Spiritism has something to say: "Life goes on in an ethereal realm, like the ghost that still lingers into the future."

Dr. J. Winston Pearce has said, "It is possible for us to stand on the wrong side of Easter and look at the cross all our lives and never be redeemed. The significance of Easter is the power of Christ's resurrection . . . every redeemed person is a testimony to the resurrection."

We live two thousand years this side of the cross, two thousand years this side of an empty tomb, and if you have not believed in Jesus Christ as Saviour, then He might as well be in that tomb as far as you are concerned. Don't put your hopes in this earthly, decaying body, but rather hope for the tabernacle of God to come. For this body will die, but the person will never die. Do you believe this?

Belief in the resurrection is vital. If Christ is Lord of life, death, hell, and the grave, the resurrection is an ethical demand. "If thou shalt confess with thy mouth the Lord Jesus," we read in Romans, "and shalt believe in thine heart that God hath raised him from the dead, thou shalt be saved" (10:9). The Bible says we must confess and believe.

Do you believe that you can live forever? Jesus declared that you can: "Verily, verily, I say unto you, The hour is coming, and now is, when the dead shall hear the voice of the Son of God: and they that hear shall live" (John 5:25). And Jesus Christ is the authority on resurrection.

"Marvel not at this," He told His disciples; ". . . all that are in the graves . . . shall come forth; they that have done good, unto the resurrection of life; and they that have done evil, unto the resurrection of damnation" (John 5:28, 29).

Peter Marshall, in a beautiful message called "Because He Rose," said:

Here is Someone who knows what He is talking about.
Here is One speaking with authority.
He has done it for others already . . .
He did it for Himself . . .
He has done it . . .
He can do it again.

AMEN!

3—SALVATION:

The Master's Mission

Jesus said, *"For the Son of man is come to seek and to save that which was lost."*

Luke 19:10

A young man named Charles G. Finney had just finished his studies for a law degree and was preparing to take his bar examination. The judge under whom he had been studying asked young Finney, "What do you plan to do now?"

"Go back to my hometown and start a law practice."

"Fine, and what will you do after that?"

"When I get established, I hope to marry and raise a family."

"And what then?"

"I'd like to obtain some of the things that will be useful to my family and beneficial to society. Maybe I'll seek a public office."

"Fine, and what then?"

"Well, I suppose I will grow old and die."

"Ah," said the old scholar, "and what then?"

Charles Finney said he was never able to get away from those words. He recognized the truth of the question, "After death, what then?" and how that question should motivate a man's life and involvements. Finney gained a life mission from that interview; he became a famous evangelist.

What about Jesus? What was Jesus Christ's mission in life? Why did God send Him into the world?

No one is truly interested in the mission of Christ until he realizes his own lostness. We may think of Jesus as a great rabbi, a great physician, a great miracle worker. We may think of Him as a great friend, but when we recognize our lost condition, we are interested in His mission here on earth.

"Atheism is an invention of modern man," said an explorer and missionary. "You will not find it among pagans and savages. I have known many tribes, and I found in each some effort toward a god, some attempt to establish a form of worship."

But none of them have found a truly satisfying religion. Only God Himself could understand man's deepest needs and provide a way of meeting them.

E. Stanley Jones, when he was a pastor, was trying to comfort a lad who had lost his father. It had been some days since the funeral, and the young fellow still had not been able to express his feelings. The kindly pastor was in the boy's bedroom, and on the chest of drawers was a picture of the family.

"I see that you are looking at your father's picture," the preacher said.

"Oh," the boy burst out, "how I wish my father could step down out of that picture!" It was a desperate cry.

That is also the need of a dying, desolate world. But God the Father has stepped down, in the person of Jesus Christ. "And the Word was made flesh, and dwelt among us," we read in John 1:14.

After His baptism and temptation, Jesus came back to His hometown and spoke in the synagogue at Nazareth. It could be called His first sermon, His inaugural address.

In actuality, it was his listeners' emancipation proclamation. But the truth of the matter was that the people preferred to remain tied down to their familiar rituals—"Having a form of godliness, but denying the power thereof . . ." (2 Timothy 3:5).

These people, like us, were used to the way things were and did not feel any need to have them drastically changed.

A prison chaplain said that in the course of establishing relationships with the prisoners, he was asked by the warden to read, in an assembly, the names of those pardoned by the governor. Usually when the chaplain spoke in assembly, the men seemed to resent it. That day the chaplain announced that he had been given permission to read the names of five men who had been granted pardons by the governor. What a difference! What attention! The convicts listened quietly and eagerly—not a word, scarcely a whisper, barely a movement while he read the names.

"It was an exhilarating moment," he reported. "As soon as I went back to my office, I realized that every time I preach, I preach pardon. Every time I preach, I proclaim that God is willing to give salvation to whomever will receive it." Those five convicts did not reject the pardon that was offered them, but eagerly received it. Too often we preach the pardon of Jesus Christ as though we feel that men do not want to know about it, do not wish to receive it.

Standing up in the synagogue at Nazareth, Jesus turned in the scroll of the Scriptures to the 61st chapter of Isaiah and began to read. On that occasion He declared the purpose of His life. Notice with whom He identifies Himself.

"The Spirit of the Lord is upon me," He read, "because he hath anointed me to preach the gospel to the poor . . ." (Luke 4:18). As the Anointed One, He proclaimed this mercy of the Father.

Anytime the church moves from the streets of the poor to green grass, it does not relocate, it dislocates. When the church moves out, crime moves in. Jesus involved Himself with the common people. He pictured His own activity in the parable of the great supper: ". . . Go out quickly into the streets and lanes of the city, and bring in hither the poor, and the maimed, and the halt, and the blind" (Luke 14:21).

In accomplishing God's plan, what was the Master's motive, His message, His method?

The Master's Motive

God's love was *the Master's motive.*

Many years ago, the first message I tried to preach was on Luke 19:10: "For the Son of man is come to seek and to save that which was lost." That is why He came. He did not come to establish a school or even a church that taught the truths of God. His chief purpose was not to establish an orphanage or a soup kitchen. He came to set up a fellowship that would have a relationship of love for Him and for one another and would care for those who were unfortunate. Other things were the result of seeking the lost, His highest motive.

The great London preacher, Charles H. Spurgeon, established an orphanage because there were so many in his congregation who died and left homeless children. On visitation day, he would go and watch for the children who didn't have anyone visiting them. One day he watched a little boy who was putting on an angry look but had tears in his eyes and was biting his lip.

"Son, what is wrong with you?" the fatherly preacher asked, as if he didn't know. The little boy looked up at him defiantly.

"How would you feel if you never had anybody to come and visit you? How would you feel if you never had anybody to bring you anything? How would you feel?"

By that time, Spurgeon was trying to wrap the little boy up in his arms, but the child pulled away rebelliously. "How would you feel if nobody loved you?"

Remember that ". . . we have not an high priest which cannot be touched with the feeling of our infirmities" (Hebrews 4:15). He feels as we feel, suffers as we suffer, hungers as we hunger. He knows all about life, and we should be comforted because we know He is alongside us in whatever we bear. To Him, we are never the untouchables.

Those who love us may slip away from us, but Jesus said, "I will never leave thee, nor forsake thee" (Hebrews 13:5). That is, "I will not leave you as orphans." Others may go away, but He does not ever have to leave us. God's people ought to feel that there is someone who loves them, because Christ has shown how much God does love us. Jesus Himself is the greatest proof, and we should have no other reason to ask God if He loves us.

Jesus did not try to establish a home for Himself—rather, a church home for us all. He talked mostly of a home with the Father over there and said, "I go to prepare a place for you" (John 14:2). We remember Him as a miracle worker and great physician, but most of all as a great Saviour, not just a great teacher. You can't dilute the fact that He said, "I am come to seek and to save that which was lost." (*See* Luke 19:10.)

Had He come to perform miracles, He could have delegated that to His disciples and bestowed on them the power. Had He come just to preach, He could have given that to Simon Peter, who later preached magnificently. Had He come just to write, He could have assigned that to the apostle Paul, for Paul wrote much of the New Testament.

Jesus came for only one reason: To save all the world—everyone who would accept Him. No one else could do that! The Bible says that ". . . there is none other name under heaven given among men, whereby we must be saved" (Acts 4:12). Only the Name of Jesus.

John the Baptist announced, "Behold the Lamb of God, which taketh away the sin of the world" (John 1:29). Jesus became identified with life for those whom men disowned and disqualified, and, it seems, especially those the Jewish leaders rejected.

For example, Zacchaeus, whose story we read in Luke 19:1–10: This little man was a publican, probably a Roman citizen although a Jew. His fellow citizens despised him and the Jews hated him. Because he worked for the Romans, he was considered a moral leper, an outcast of society, by the Jews. The priests of that day wrote him off. Jesus came to his house and wrote him down in the Lamb's Book of Life.

Approaching Jericho, Jesus looked up into a tree and said, "Come down, Zacchaeus. This day I'll eat at your house."

That was only Jesus' preliminary invitation. He could not give Zacchaeus salvation unless the man wanted it. But Jesus reached out to him. He reached up to him, as well. It had been a long time since Zacchaeus had received a kind word, and he melted like a child. Many criticized Jesus for having dinner with Zacchaeus, but not many of them were trying to win a lost world or to save sinners. They were just saying how *they* would do it.

There was no starch in the hem of Jesus' garment. He moved among the people, and wherever He went, He searched out the needy. As we search our own lives, aren't we glad that He claimed the disowned? Otherwise, we would have no place in His service.

The Master's Message

We need to consider not only the Master's motive but *the Master's message*—God's message through Him. It is the message of hope, the message of salvation—the Gospel. Often we hear people talk about preaching the Gospel of Jesus Christ when they can't even define it.

"What is the Gospel?" we ask. "Is it just preaching against cigarette smoking, for instance?" No, the Gospel of Christ is *not* preaching against anything—it is the *Good News.* It is the Good News that God loves you enough to send His Son, Jesus Christ, into the world to die for you.

If ever there was a man who should not have had to suffer, it was Jesus. But He suffered that we might be able to go free. He died for all people, the up and outs as well as the down and outs—also those with the ups and downs. He didn't just tell us what was wrong with us, but how we could get right.

In John 3:7 we find Jesus with tenderness, without apology, but with absolute authority, telling Nicodemus, "Ye must be born again."

He made no exceptions. He didn't say, "It's all right if you believe differently from Me." He didn't tell the priests, "I recognize that you have your traditions; if you feel that you had better go on in the same way, it is all right."

Jesus turned to Nicodemus, representative of the intellectual who was disenchanted with all that he had been taught, all that he had memorized, and all that he had practiced, and told him he must be born again. Nicodemus had absolutely no joy in his practice of religion. He knew the laws of Moses; he knew the detailed regulations of the sacrifices; he understood the rules of personal behavior. Laws he understood, yet somehow, love had never grasped him.

Was not that the reason Nicodemus came to Jesus and said, ". . . Rabbi, we know that thou art a teacher come from God" (John 3:2). Here was a man of morals and religion, but not a Christian. Everything that he knew sounded good, but it wouldn't do for dying. If it won't do for dying, it really isn't any good for living, either.

The famous author O. Henry said something that surely he didn't intend should be written down. Just as death began to overtake him, he said to his nurse, "Turn up the lights . . . ." He didn't want to die in the dark!

In Jesus' day, the prophets had been silent for many centuries. The priests killed sacrificial lambs on God's altar more out of ritual than out of real worship. For 400 years there had been no word from God, and the desperate cry of a lost world was, "O God, pull up the shades. We don't want to die in the dark!"

That was why the aged Simeon in the temple said, as he held the baby Jesus, "Lord, now lettest thou thy servant depart in peace . . . For mine eyes have seen thy salvation" (Luke 2:29, 30).

Jesus said, "I am the light of the world," and a songwriter, Philip P. Bliss, has repeated it:

The whole world was lost in the darkness of sin;
The Light of the world is Jesus!

"Permit me to write the music of a nation," said a wise man, "and I will let others write its laws." Music influences lives, and singing has always played a large part in Christian worship. The Gospel is something to sing about.

When Horace Bushnell was a student at Yale, he claimed to be an atheist. His teacher asked him what he believed, and Bushnell answered, "I don't believe anything!" Finally he admitted he was feeling depressed. "I do believe in truth."

"Then I have nothing to worry about," the teacher said, and relaxed. "Because if you really believe in truth, then you will come to seek even His truth."

Although that young Yale student went other paths and tried other ways, there came a time when Horace Bushnell did grasp for the Gospel—and it was because he searched for truth. Eventually he became a great preacher and a well-known Christian educator.

When men are searching for truth and peace, it is actually *life* and *truth* in search of them. "I am the way, the truth, and the life," Jesus said.

George Whitefield said about the repentant thief on the cross that he was the reject of society, the devil's castaway. He had been found guilty in the courts of men—completely dishonored. In utter desperation, but with childlike faith, he turned to Jesus and said, "O Lord, remember me." Sometimes we forget that Jesus did not die on the sacramental table between two calves; He died on the cross between two thieves. And in the last moments of life, one dishonored thief made Jesus' cross a stepping-stone to salvation.

Only relatively few words in the Gospels tell the story of the cross. Who would have told it as the Gospel writers wrote it? The account has to be true, because nobody would have imagined it as it was written. We wouldn't have the disciples leaving Jesus as He hung on the cross; we wouldn't have Him die an ignominious death there. We would have made a hero out of Him. But we didn't have a hero until the resurrection. Death has no heroes.

His disciples, brokenhearted, went their separate

ways, going to sleep that night in restless beds, for it seemed that their Master had been dishonored and disowned by God. He had cried out, "My God, my God, why hast thou forsaken me?" (Matthew 27:46).

God's method of getting things done is far different from any ideas of ours. Jesus Christ's message was predetermined by God before the foundation of the world and recorded in the early part of the Bible. "And I will put enmity between thee and the woman," God told Satan, "and between thy seed and her seed; it shall bruise thy head, and thou shalt bruise his heel" (Genesis 3:15).

The Master's Method

What was *the Master's method?* In the first place, it was intensely personal. He always ministered to the individual. Every day, house to house, person to person—no one was exempt from His invitation. Jesus Christ never deviated from His purpose.

"He never failed in private," Alexander Maclaren said of Christ, "save once, and that was with Pilate. He never succeeded in public save once, and that was at Calvary." Jesus was interested in ministering to people of all types.

He ministered to the disabled. In Luke 4:18—"He hath sent me to heal . . . and recovering of sight to the blind," Jesus read from the Book of Isaiah. To the lame, to the blind, the name of Jesus brought hope of recovery. Blind Bartimaeus thrilled with joy when he heard Jesus' name called, and "received his sight" (*see* Mark

10:46). On another occasion, Jesus made room for a lame man who was lowered through the ceiling by four of his friends.

Christ ministered to the disillusioned. "He hath sent me . . . to set at liberty them that are bruised" (Luke 4:18).

A woman of Samaria who had lost all faith in society came to draw water at "Jacob's well" in the noonday sun. When, suprisingly, Jesus, a stranger to her, spoke, she demanded suspiciously, "What do you want of me?" She had never been able to trust anyone; why should she trust this man?

"Give me water" was what Jesus had said to her.

She turned on Him with bitterness, and because of this bitterness, she nearly missed the way. He who was *the* Way was interrupted by one who didn't know the way. Everyone else had *taken* from her, but Christ had come to *give* ". . . a well of water springing up into everlasting life" (John 4:14).

Finally, with loving understanding, Jesus told her all the things that she had ever done—not to embarrass her, but to show her His way—to convict her.

Why was she disillusioned? Jesus described the cause well when He said, "Ye worship ye know not what . . ." (John 4:22). In other words, "You don't know how to worship or where to worship, and you do not know whom you worship." It is no wonder the woman was confused and gone astray. Her faith in God was muddled with prejudice and tradition. That day Jesus restored her faith with His caring love. To the confused and disillusioned He brought hope.

Because some may send us on our way, we sometimes get confused and apologetic. We never even get their attention. But just remember, they don't know what to worship or where to worship—they are always giving an excuse—they have no real apology. But we must persist with concern and compassion; our example is Jesus Himself.

The Master's method was to take broken-down people and rebuild their lives on a new foundation. The Gospel is most readily heard by the poor, the brokenhearted, the captive, the blind, and the bruised.

There are many passages in the Scriptures telling us more of the Master's mission in His own words. Let us see what He did *not* come to do: "Think not that I am come to destroy the law, or the prophets . . . but to fulfil" (Matthew 5:17). "I am not come to call the righteous, but sinners to repentance" (Matthew 9:13). "The Son of man came not to be ministered unto, but to minister, and to give his life a ransom for many" (Mark 10:45).

Then Jesus also stated His purpose in the positive: "For the Son of man is come to save that which was lost" (Matthew 18:11). "I am come a light into the world, that whosoever believeth on me should not abide in darkness" (John 12:46). Christ came bearing the Good News. In a nutshell, He stated the Gospel as: "I am come that they might have life, and that they might have it more abundantly" (John 10:10).

The apostle Paul outlined the points in 1 Corinthians 15:3, 4: "For I delivered unto you first of all that which I also received, how that Christ died for our sins according to the scriptures; And that he was buried, and that he rose again the third day according to the scriptures."

A disabled man had four friends who brought him to Jesus and put him down in front of the Master. When bystanders criticized Jesus' method of healing, He replied, "Which is more difficult, to say, Rise, take up thy bed and walk, or, Thy sins be forgiven thee?" (*See* Luke 5:23.)

When His mission was completed, Jesus said, "[Father] I have glorified thee on the earth: I have finished the work which thou gavest me to do" (John 17:4).

The apostle Paul summarized Jesus' work, His mission: "For ye know the grace of our Lord Jesus Christ, that, though he was rich, yet for your sakes he became poor, that ye through his poverty might be rich" (2 Corinthians 8:9).

4—HEAVEN:
The Realm of the Redeemed

Jesus said: *"I go to prepare a place for you."*

John 14:2

Many glorious experiences in life we dismiss with a rueful remark: "All good things must come to an end." But that is not true! The most perfect and wonderful thing in the world—salvation—begins in the human breast by faith and has its climactic experience in the presence of Almighty God forever and ever.

Certainly it is not true of heaven that all good things come to an end. For if we now have a heavenly spirit and a heavenly vision, we shall one day have the heavenly experience. And it will never end. How sublime heaven will be! It is almost more than we can possibly think about. One joyous part of our faith includes the promises God has clearly revealed concerning heaven. We couldn't keep our faith if it were not for the promises of the Bible.

Jesus realized how necessary it was for Him to reassure His disciples when they became disturbed over the prospect of His going away from them. "Let not your heart be troubled," He told them, "ye believe in God, believe also in me . . . . I go to prepare a place for you" (John 14:1, 2).

The disciples recognized that Jesus had all power, but the thought that He would be absent from their sight was upsetting. They began to question, and the long discourses of John, chapters 14 through 17, contain His explanations.

The apostle Paul made a great statement which can be colloquially translated, "It is far more better to be with Christ, far more better to be with Him in His presence who has ascended up into heaven." (*See* Philippians 1:23.) Yet even the early Christians did not fully recognize this.

Earth is a very tangible place, but it is insecure and fleeting. Jesus said it is to pass away, while heaven is permanent and eternal. To a Christian, heaven represents the very goal of life and should give meaning to life. If all we have to look forward to in this life is despair, disease, and decay, there is not much to live for. But by telling us about heaven, Christ gave richer meaning to life here.

"I have set before you life and death . . ." said an ancient prophet, "therefore choose life" (Deuteronomy 30:19). Jesus said, "Because strait is the gate, and narrow is the way, which leadeth unto life, and few there be that find it" (Matthew 7:14). The Way is clearly marked by the Word of God, that there might be no mistake.

Let it never be forgotten that a sense of destiny determines a man's character. What he believes about the future has something to do with how he behaves in the present. Sometimes we have more mental believers than we have moral behavers. The man who has lost all sight of spiritual things has no heavenly vision.

Even those who talk much of heaven may not be properly prepared. Unfortunately, what the old spiritual says is true: "Everybody talking 'bout heaven ain't going there!" What we believe about heaven must be founded upon the Bible. That wonderful Word of God tells us that heaven is a prepared place, a perfect place, a place of privilege.

A Prepared Place

Jesus told His disciples that heaven is *a prepared place:* "In my Father's house are many mansions: if it were not so, I would have told you. I go to prepare a place for you. And if I go and prepare a place for you, I will come again, and receive you unto myself; that where I am, there ye may be also" (John 14:2, 3).

Billy Graham has written in *Decision* magazine, "I personally believe the Bible teaches that heaven is a literal place . . . . heaven is going to be home . . . . heaven is going to be a place of service . . . . Heaven will be a place where all mysteries are cleared up." We have many mysteries here and have pondered the strangeness of life. We've sat in quiet places and wondered about many conditions, many experiences. But when we come into the presence of God, these things will be cleared up.

Heaven is a place prepared for the pure in heart. Jesus said in the Beatitudes: "Blessed are the pure in heart: for they shall see God" (Matthew 5:8). Heaven truly is a prepared place for a prepared people.

Heaven is not prepared for the man who has sin in his life, because a man who clings to his sins would not enjoy heaven. The Garden of Eden could not have remained perfect; it could no longer be heaven on earth for Adam and Eve after they had sinned. They began to want more and more. There was the further potential for sin in their lives, even in that perfect paradise prepared by God Himself. Everything was good in the sight of God; everything was fashioned right, except that Adam and Eve chose sin and there could be no heaven where there was sin.

To the minds of Jesus' disciples, His words about heaven must have seemed a great mystery. But surely Jesus' words were infallible. Much later, He ascended into heaven before their eyes, beyond and away from human sight.

Heaven is a prepared place because it is a place of great expectations. Jesus was a builder from the beginning. During His earthly life, He worked in Joseph's carpenter shop in Nazareth. But He did not take His real apprenticeship there. He did not learn how to build things there. He learned how to build in the office of the Supreme Architect of the whole universe. When the stars were flung into space, Jesus was there. When the oceans were rolled back and the land formed into continents, Jesus was there. When all the animals were shaped, Jesus was there.

When man was created in the image of God, Jesus was there. "All things were made by him," John wrote, "and without him was not any thing made that was made" (John 1:3). He is the Supreme Architect of earth and heaven itself, though with human hands He smoothed the ox yoke.

Now He who designed all we find good and beautiful

here has gone to heaven to make a home for you and me. Who could visualize anything better than what the Supreme Architect of the ages will prepare for us? It is more wonderful than we can imagine. "Eye hath not seen, nor ear heard, neither have entered into the heart of man, the things which God has prepared for them that love him" (1 Corinthians 2:9).

A Perfect Place

Jesus said heaven is *a perfect place*. There will be nothing unsightly; there will be no discord; there will be no discrepancies. It will be perfect in the sight of God.

Do you realize that now He is preparing *you* for the place He has already prepared *for* you? He is trying to get us ready—sometimes in spite of ourselves. Right now He is preparing you for heaven: molding and shaping you in the image of Almighty God.

Therefore heaven is not only a prepared place, but it is a perfect place, because He will be there. ". . . I will come again, and receive you unto myself; that where I am, there ye may be also" (John 14:3). That one statement answers everything the Christian needs to know. Heaven is homecoming; heaven is being with Jesus.

Near the end of the Book of Revelation you will find several *no more*s about heaven. First, "There will be no more sea"—that is, nothing that separates. (*See* Revelation 21:1.) Never again shall any child of God be separated from the presence of God. As Christians, we have been separated *into* the presence of God, not from Him. He will remove us from this world to that perfect place He has prepared for us.

Also, "There shall be no more death, neither sorrow, nor crying, neither shall there be any more pain" (Revelation 21:4). How wonderful that there will be no sickness there! How much of the ministry of the church is involved with sickness and death! The two things that we are most often dealing with in life are getting people ready to live and getting people ready to die. That's what the ministry is all about. But Jesus said that there will be no sickness and death there.

No temple will be needed in heaven, for God *is* its Temple and He is everywhere. The sun and moon will not be shining, for He is the Light, and there will be no night there. (*See* Revelation 21:22, 23.)

One thing I think of most is that there will be no more sin. "And there shall in no wise enter into it any thing that defileth, neither whatsoever worketh abomination, or maketh a lie: but they which are written in the Lamb's book of life" (21:27). Sinners, yes—sinners who have been saved by grace and made into saints. Christians are saints of God, not because of anything they have done, but because they have been justified in God's sight by the One in whom they believe.

Certainly it is very difficult for me to think in terms of being a saint. I could think of some who have gone before me, and perhaps a few contemporaries, as saints of God. Most of us have some difficulty comprehending and a lot of hesitation really thinking of ourselves under the title *saints*. Yet God has said so! We can scarcely believe it, but then we shall experience it. "And there shall be no more curse . . ." (22:3). There will be no sin in heaven—that you can count on.

But there will be saved sinners—many, many of them! Heaven will be a populated place. You might have the most wonderful garden in all the world, with the most beautiful varieties of birds singing there, but if nobody is around and God is not there, that wouldn't be heaven as far as I am concerned. A garden wouldn't be meaningful without people to enjoy it.

The Bible does not indicate that heaven will be a lonely place, because God Himself hungered for fellowship. Even after He made the world and saw that things were perfect in the animal and vegetable kingdoms, there was an emptiness. So God made man. He made man out of a desperate need for fellowship, for He made man in His own image. Man is fashioned after God—not this body, but that spark of divinity that God placed in man. There is something about man that is different from the animals. Is it not the soul of man, the spirit of man, the conscious life of man, that is in the image of God?

Heaven, to *be* heaven, has to be a populated place. It is prepared for a great many people, not just a few. Of course, it sometimes seems that not many folks are heaven bound. But we must recognize that "we also are compassed about with so great a cloud of witnesses" (Hebrews 12:1). There are those who have gone before us and there are those who will go with us and there are those who will come behind us.

What else will be different about this perfect place? Will we know one another there?

We have a right to believe, by the teachings of the Scriptures, that heaven will be a place of perfection and all imperfection shall be lost with this earthly body.

D. L. Moody pointed out that we recognize one another down here, and in heaven we shall certainly be no less intelligent.

Here we have imperfect sight, but there we shall have perfect sight. "For now we see through a glass, darkly; but then face to face . . ." (1 Corinthians 13:12). For all we think we see in this life, we see only partially. Then we will see all things perfectly.

A friend of mine, one of the former presidents of the Southern Baptist Convention, said he knew a minister who had lived to be almost ninety years of age and had been blind all his life. My friend, because he recognized that the elderly man was not long for this life, went to see him. He sat by the bed.

"Do you realize," the aged man said, "I have never seen you in all these years I have known you, ever since you were a boy?" With sensitive fingers, he began to feel: the nose, the head, the face. "It is not going to be long now until I will see you—but do you know whom I will see first?"

"Yes," the younger preacher said, not having an easy time with his emotions or finding a way to put them into words.

The older man's face shone with joy about his home going: "The first face I shall see is Jesus! To tell you the truth, it is nearly worth being blind for ninety years just to get to see Jesus first of all. The first thing—the very first face I shall really see—is the face of Jesus!"

The truth of the matter is, for all of us, the first one we will *really* see is Jesus. We think we see other things and people. We ask if our loved ones will be the same. I don't think so; I don't believe heaven will be a static condition. That doesn't worry me, because we won't be the same, either. Have you thought about that? When your loved ones go away for a time on this earth, you don't stand still, and neither do they.

Life does not stop because of separation. It goes on, and hopefully, every year we grow more godlike. Even here, as you learn a little more about the Lord, you grow more easily recognizable as a Christian because you favor your Father. On the Mount of Transfiguration Jesus' three disciples evidently recognized Moses and Elijah without an introduction, although they had never met them.

Recognition should not be a problem. Don't you think the great God, who made us for the first time, will be able to grasp our needs and essence and remake us and blend us into absolute perfection?

Heaven is a perfect place because there is room enough. "In my Father's house are many mansions . . ." Jesus said (John 14:2). It is paradoxical that here we didn't have room for Him when He came, but He is making much room for us. We turned Him aside, but He is waiting to welcome us.

Literally, the *many mansions* should be translated "a place of many rooms, or a dwelling place." If you do not have a place in heaven, it is because you will not find room in your heart for Jesus here. That is the only reason! It is not because of His inability or His lack of capacity, but because you refuse to give Him room.

Joseph and Mary came to Bethlehem and were denied room. There was no room for them in the inn. "But whosoever shall deny me before men," Jesus said, "him will I also deny before my Father which is in heaven" (Matthew 10:33). But whoever will confess Him before men, He declared, "I will confess his name before my Father, and before his angels" (Revelation 3:5).

There will be no place for you in heaven without an advance reservation. The recording angel has dipped his pen in the blood of the Lamb, as it were, and we are to "rejoice, because your names are written in heaven" (Luke 10:20).

If heaven is a perfect place, it must be a real place, rather than a figment of the imagination. It has to be a real place, or there would have been no place for Jesus to go in His resurrected body when He ascended up into heaven. He couldn't hide in the clouds. He was in a body, and there must be a place for that body. And it has to be a perfect place, to be worthy of the Son of God.

A Privileged Place

Certainly heaven is also *a privileged place;* it will be our greatest glory to be there. And Christ alone is the door into that permanent paradise.

How do you gain the privilege of being in heaven? ". . . I am the way, the truth, and the life," Christ said, "no man cometh unto the Father, but by me" (John 14:6). Christ is the Way; faith is the key; death is the door. There is no way for you to go to heaven except through the portals of death, unless Christ should come back before you die and catch you up to be with Him.

What a privilege, what a joy it will be to stand with the saints of God there!

When He shall call, from earth's remotest corners
All who have stood triumphant in His might,
Oh, to be worthy then to stand before Him
And in that hour to walk with them in white.

Almeda J. Pearce

The first glimpse a man had of heaven, according to the Bible, was when Jacob saw a ladder to heaven and "angels of God ascending and descending on it" (Genesis 28:12). As he pillowed his head on a stone, he heard a voice speaking the promise of God from the top of the ladder: "And, behold, I am with thee, and will keep thee in all places whither thou goest . . ." (Genesis 28:15).

Heaven was also opened to Stephen. As he was being stoned to death, he said, "Behold, I see the heavens opened, and the Son of man standing on the right hand of God" (Acts 7:56). It wasn't a delusion, it was a heavenly vision, a glimpse of glory.

Paul had a vision, also. "I knew a man . . . (whether in the body, I cannot tell; or whether out of the body, I cannot tell: God knoweth;) such an one caught up into the third heaven . . . . and heard unspeakable words, which it is not lawful for a man to utter" (2 Corinthians 12:2, 4).

In other words, if I had the absolutely perfect vision of heaven, what man of imperfect vision would believe me? Who would believe what Paul was trying to say?

We don't have anything except our limited words and limited experiences by which to describe heavenly things. How are you going to picture it with man's words and material terms and symbols? We think of gold and silver and pearls. Paul said, "I saw things unlawful for me to utter."

But as Jesus Himself foretold in a parable, if we belong to Him, surely we will be welcomed by His outstretched hands, in which are yet the marks of the nail prints. "Come, ye blessed of my Father," He will say, "inherit the kingdom prepared for you before the foundation of the world" (Matthew 25:34).

5—SATAN:
The Defeated Destroyer

Jesus said: *"I beheld Satan as lightning fall from heaven."*

Luke 10:18

Is the devil for real? What do you think?

Martin Luther, that great kindler of the Reformation, believed with all his heart that the devil was real. It is said that one day in his study he felt the presence of the devil so strongly that he threw an inkwell from his desk at the corner in which it seemed to him the devil stood.

At the other extreme, there are those who say that Satan is a principle rather than a person, an influence rather than a presence.

Certainly Satan is a power, but far more than that. His most effective delusion is persuading us to doubt him or to believe that good and evil are simply principles. Good and evil are principles, of course, but they are focused, or personified, if you will, in the very real personalities of God and Satan. It has been said that if you take the *d* from *devil,* you get *evil,* and if you put an *o* in *God,* you get *good.*

In *Old Testament Outline Studies,* W. E. Moorehead made the interesting statement: "It is noteworthy that nearly all the revelation we have of this great evil spirit is found in the New Testament. Rarely is he mentioned in the Old—in Eden [Genesis 3:1–15], in Job [1–2], David [1 Chronicles 21:1], and Joshua the High Priest [Zechariah 3:2]. God delayed the full disclosure of him to later times, and then gave him 28 names which fully describe him."

One of the names given to him is Deceiver. Another of Satan's shrewdest stunts is persuading us to laugh at him and not take him seriously. He is pleased when we chuckle at the ridiculous idea of a bogeyman with horns and a forked tail. He would prefer that we think of him in Halloween context; a phantom to be resurrected in costumes for parties and held up to laughter. But he cannot be laughed off. In fact, he cannot be washed off, even with tears. Only the blood of Christ can challenge him and destroy him.

Jesus Christ never minimized the devil or laughed at him. "Naturally, what he said as to Satan's nature and activities," wrote Dr. Herbert Lockyer, "form only a part—withal a most vital part—of the full portrait of the enemy of God and of man. Yet while the Master's unfolding of Satan is limited in scope, it will be found that all he did say about him is everywhere essentially consistent with what the rest of Scripture records as to his character."

If the presence of Satan was experienced in a very real way by Jesus, certainly he will be experienced in our lives, also. "Your adversary, the devil," as Peter called him in 1 Peter 5:8, is mentioned in almost a hundred passages of Scripture.

The Bible doesn't define God, or explain God, but rather proclaims Him. Neither does the Bible explain Satan or the presence of evil, but rather presents him as a personality to be reckoned with in human history. We should not study about the devil as an object of curiosity, but seek information from God's Word so that we might know how to face this powerful foe. The Bible is full of warnings against him and his devices.

Satan is the archenemy of God, and quite clearly the avowed enemy of every soul. "And fear not them which kill the body, but are not able to kill the soul," Jesus warned, "but rather fear him which is able to destroy both soul and body in hell" (Matthew 10:28).

In the days of Job, God asked Satan, "Where have you been?"

"Walking to and fro among God's people," the devil replied. (*See* Job 1:7.) He still spends his time doing that. A preacher named Carleton said, "The service has started, and unnoticed but always present is Satan, as he was with Job."

What do we learn about Satan in the Bible? When did he make his debut in human history? What is his design for this world? Thank God, he will be defeated in it!

The Devil's Debut

Let us look at *the devil's debut,* his appearance in this world. We cannot be sure of the exact origin of Satan, but there are several passages that shed light on his fall. You can see his tracks through time, from the very beginning of Genesis, through Revelation, and to this present hour.

In Genesis, we encounter Satan for the first time in the Garden of Eden, talking to Eve. He must have seemed beautiful in her sight, with the glory of his angelic origin. But sin came into this world through Satan and his rebellion. The sin of Adam and Eve was the first sin of mankind, but not the first sin against God.

"The fact that Satan did fall," said A. W. Pink, "is proof that God did not create the devil, but created the one who became the devil." It seems likely that God created Lucifer as an archangel, but he fell because of his pride.

> How art thou fallen from heaven, O Lucifer, son of the morning! how art thou cut down to the ground, which didst weaken the nations! For thou hast said in thine heart . . . I will exalt my throne above the stars of God . . . I will be like the Most High.
>
> Isaiah 14:12–14

This is a vivid picture of the sin of pride.

Angels were not made robots; they were given free will, even as men were given free will. God created them to serve, but evidently Satan rebelled against his subordinate position. And there are some devilish acts today of people rebelling against the service of Almighty God.

In the Bible two kinds of angels are mentioned: those who serve and glorify God and those who are fallen. There were some—and their leader was Satan—who in their pride raised themselves up against God and would not worship Him. Jude 6 speaks of "the angels which kept not their first estate, but left their own habitation, he hath reserved in everlasting chains under darkness unto the judgment of the great day." They left the place for which God created them, becoming both originators and victims of sin.

Revelation 12:7–9 records a war in heaven in which the host of angels were cast out, and in Luke 10:18 Jesus said, "I beheld Satan as lightning fall from heaven."

In the Scriptures, the devil is referred to by several names: Deceiver, Destroyer, Lucifer, Satan, and many others. Forty titles altogether are given to him. *Satan* means "adversary" and *devil* means "slanderer." Certainly he demonstrates all the attributes of personality which go far beyond mere influence. There is evidence of intelligence, memory, speech, will and emotion. We can see all these things in the eighty-nine times he is mentioned in the Scriptures.

Near the end of Jesus' ministry, He said to Simon Peter, "Satan hath desired to have you, that he may sift you as wheat" (Luke 22:31). This certainly reflects emotion on the part of Satan, one of the major attributes of personality.

From the Scriptures and from personal encounter, we must confess that we believe in a powerful and personal devil. He made his debut to mankind in the Garden of Eden, but he began as a creation of God in eternity past.

The Devil's Design

Now let us look at *the devil's design.* What purpose does he have in this world?

Jesus warned Peter that the greatest devilish delight,

Satan's greatest desire, is the sifting of the saints of God.

Before God's throne, Satan always appears in his true light, because God knows him as he is. But before men his design is one of disguise. Satan is the great imposter and counterfeiter of all time. He mimics everything that is good.

Satan's activities include distraction, disturbance, and deceit. You can be sure that wherever distraction is, whether as riots in the streets or side issues in the church, the devil is the author of it. We say, "Where there's smoke there is bound to be fire"—but don't be too sure! Satan has been making smoke without fire for a long, long time.

"If I were the devil," Roy McClain once said, "I would make people believe that religion is something dull and tasteless and not very vital."

One of Satan's tools is slander. He slanders God to men and he slanders men to God. He did this in the case of Job. "Doth Job fear God for nought?" he insinuated in Job 1:9. In other words, "God, You are paying him to be good. If You took his possessions, family, and health from him, he would deny You to Your face."

The devil slandered Job—and he slanders all men—to God.

Satan slandered God to man when he said to Eve, "For God doth know that in the day ye eat thereof, then your eyes shall be opened, and ye shall be as gods, knowing good and evil" (Genesis 3:5). He wanted Eve to believe that God wasn't being quite fair with her, not to let her have everything that she desired. His design includes malicious slander.

Satan's position is always that of an adversary, a prosecuting attorney. He tempts both man and God. Don't think that you and I will be any exception, for if he tempted Jesus in the flesh, you can be sure that he will continually tempt us in our flesh. "Put on the whole armour of God," Paul implored the Ephesians, "that ye may be able to stand against the wiles of the devil" (6:11).

The power of Satan is real; sometimes it seems that we are in his clutches to the degree that there is no way out. One addicted to the bottle would say so. The one addicted to drugs would say so. They are being made fools of by Satan. These are satanic things, but God set a limit upon the power of Satan, not only in the future, but now.

In a parable, Jesus pictured Satan as a strong man, who cannot be deprived of his possessions unless he is first bound. (*See* Mark 3:27.) This Christ has done. Satan has only a time lease of activity. The Book of Job shows that Satan is like a dog on a leash and cannot go further than divine permission will allow him to go.

For as Satan charged God concerning Job, "Hast not thou made an hedge about him?" (Job 1:10).

God replied, "Behold, all that he hath is in thy power; only upon himself put not forth thine hand" (v. 12). In other words, "You can touch him. But only under certain conditions. You can't touch his soul."

Satan's method is one of hindrance. There are many examples in the Scriptures of the hindrances that Satan has used. He perverts the Word of God, as when he quoted half-truths to Christ in the "wilderness of temptation."

> For it is written, He shall give his angels
> charge over thee, to keep thee: And in their
> hands they shall bear thee up, lest at any time
> thou dash thy foot against a stone.
>
> Luke 4:10, 11

He never quoted God or the Bible in its real meaning, but only in twisted half-truths.

The devil's methods include deception by "signs and lying wonders" (2 Thessalonians 2:9). In Exodus, he enabled the magicians of Egypt to duplicate some of Moses' miracles "with their enchantments: and Pharaoh's heart was hardened" (Exodus 7:22).

". . . He is a liar, and the father of it," Christ said of the devil in John 8:44. Satan has won himself a host of followers since then. Just bear in mind that you are one of the devil's disciples when you engage in lying.

The devil's strategy is carefully fitted to the person he is approaching and whatever that one's desires might be at that particular moment. Satan changes uniforms from time to time and place to place to do whatever he can to gain his ends. His blow to David was through sensual appetite; with Elijah he used despondency; in Moses' case, disobedience to God.

What is your problem? What does he use when he tempts you? Remember, he is always two-faced; he tempts us that he may accuse us. In Revelation 12:10 we read, ". . . the accuser of our brethren is cast down, which accused them before our God day and night." Without doubt, the devil is Public Enemy #1. He carries on a godless guerilla warfare, attacking stealthily and constantly. Our alertness must be unfailing.

C. S. Lewis described Satan's tactics in *The Screwtape Letters:* "If he cannot find anything else wrong, he will simply listen for the squeak in the usher's shoes. If he finds nothing wrong morally, then he will find something else to suit the occasion."

"[The devil] was a murderer from the beginning . . ." said Jesus (John 8:44). The word He used means *man-slayer.* This same term was used to describe one who hates his brother. (*See* 1 John 3:15.)

Satanic sabotage against the saints of God is sudden and subtle.

The Devil's Defeat

Satan's designs are endless, but there is another prospect beyond that, for which we thank God: *the devil's defeat.*

At present Satan is going about "as a roaring lion . . . seeking whom he may devour" (1 Peter 5:8). It seems that he is in possession of this earth. When Satan offered the kingdoms of the world to Jesus, the Son of God found no fault with his claim. Jesus did not tell the devil that these were not his to give.

Several times Jesus spoke of him as "the prince of this world." (*See* John 12:31; 14:30; 16:11.) In Ephesians 2:2, Paul called him "the prince of the power of the air." Sometimes it seems that Satan is in control of the church, too.

The devil seems to have the world in the palm of his hand today. He is infecting it with his ambition and selfishness and greed, inciting men to force and sinful pleasure. He should be very pleased—he seems to be able to accomplish his designs, and the children of God often seem to be in ultimate defeat—but don't be too sure. We have yet to turn over the last chapter and see the final outcome.

Let me remind you again that Satan is suffering from the terminal disease of sin! It is the disease that kills: "For the wages of sin is death . . ." (Romans 6:23). One day Satan will be bound and "cast into the lake of fire and brimstone," we read in Revelation 20:10.

Man was created in the image of God, and therefore we must be more than mere pawns in Satan's game of sifting. As you get off your knees, stand tall and recognize that if you are a child of God, He is at your side.

Christ assured Peter that He was praying for him: "But I have prayed for thee, that thy faith fail not . . ." (Luke 22:32). If He prayed for Simon Peter, you can be sure He will pray for us. In John 17:15 we read the words of Jesus to His Father, "I pray . . . that thou shouldest keep them from the evil [one, Satan]."

If we are willing to let Christ pray for us, and listen to His prayer, we can be assured that God will hear our prayer to be delivered from Satan, if we really desire it. The very familiar words of "The Lord's Prayer" include the petition, "And lead us not into temptation, but deliver us from evil" (Matthew 6:13).

Sometimes we look back at past performances and defeats and feel that Satan always wins. But read the Book of Revelation—the last chapter in Satan's story. There we find that, when Jesus Christ displays His triumph over death and the grave, Satan will be dethroned, chained, and cast into hell.

In Genesis 3:15 we have the first promise that God gave mankind, and He will keep it: "And I will put enmity between thee [Satan] and the woman, and between thy seed and her seed; it shall bruise thy head, and thou shalt bruise his heel."

When the Prince of Peace comes to reign, you can be sure that the prince of this world will be cast out.

> He that committeth sin is of the devil; for the devil sinneth from the beginning. For this purpose the Son of God was manifested, that he might destroy the works of the devil.
>
> 1 John 3:8

Hebrews 2:14 says Christ died ". . . that through death he might destroy him that had the power of death, that is, the devil."

Man can only find victory over the devil in Christ, not in his own self. Christ will be the final Victor and Ruler, and because we belong to Him, we shall share the victory that belongs to Him. Our part is to proclaim Him: ". . . to turn them [the Gentiles] from darkness to light, and from the power of Satan unto God." (*See* Acts 26:18.)

The devil's debut in this world was marked by lying and trickery. The devil's design for mankind is turmoil, rebellion, and accusation before God. Be warned, and don't go down in defeat with him. In the end, death shall be defeated and Satan destroyed. The Son of God, our Saviour, shall be Victor forever.

6—HELL:
A Great Gulf Fixed

Jesus said: *"There is a great gulf fixed."*
Luke 16:26

Winston Churchill said on one occasion that "the present moral landslide in Great Britain can be traced to the fact that heaven and hell are no longer proclaimed throughout the land." This could also be said about America. Hell is not preached simply to frighten people nor heaven just to subdue them, but rather because of the choice faced by men at the crossroads of life. The fork of the road a man chooses, whether broad or narrow, determines his destiny.

Jesus came from heaven, but certainly He was also an authority on hell. "Wide is the gate, and broad is the way, that leadeth to destruction," He said. (*See* Matthew 7:13.)

Listen to a story Jesus told: "There was a certain rich man . . . And there was a certain beggar named Lazarus . . . . And it came to pass that the beggar died, and was carried by the angels into Abraham's bosom: the rich man also died, and was buried" (Luke 16:19, 20, 22).

That would be the end of the story as we might tell it. But Jesus knew what lay beyond death.

> And in hell he lift up his eyes, being in torments, and seeth Abraham afar off, and Lazarus in his bosom. And he cried and said, Father Abraham, have mercy on me, and send Lazarus, that he may dip the tip of his finger in water, and cool my tongue; for I am tormented in this flame.
>
> Luke 16:23, 24

In discussing hell, we have to face one of the most stubborn, unpleasant, and universally ignored doctrines in all the Bible. In all generations, every Christian minister has had to address himself to this issue and face his people with these unwelcome facts.

How do we describe the reality of hell? What facts do we know about hell? In the Bible, we find our answers. This passage quoted from the lips of Jesus presents one of the most vivid pictures we know. Here the rich man is described as "being in torments" and crying out for someone to "dip the tip of his finger in water, and cool my tongue; for I am tormented in this flame."

What was Abraham's reply?

> . . . Son, remember that thou in thy lifetime receivedst thy good things, and likewise Lazarus evil things: but now he is comforted, and thou art tormented. And beside all this, between us and you there is a great gulf fixed: so that they which would pass from hence to you cannot; neither can they pass to us, that would come from thence.
>
> Luke 16:25, 26

The willfulness of man shows up in great contrast to the love of God. Between them there is forever a great gulf fixed. Only the glorious sacrifice of Christ could build a bridge—a bridge that can be entered only from this life.

Often we hear the love of God put forth as a reason why there should not be a hell. But on the other hand, what can He do with the sinfulness of man? "The eternal punishment of the wicked is not arbitrarily imposed by God," said Dr. Herbert Lockyer, "but is the inevitable outcome of sin itself—the confirmation of sinners in their own self-chosen course, being left by God to reap the full, dire consequences of sin."

How can we even think about the love of God without recognizing our sinfulness? The very nearness of God makes us aware of sin.

Hell was not prepared for God's children; it was not designed for men at all. Jesus Himself described hell as an "everlasting fire, prepared for the devil and his angels" (Matthew 25:41). The devil's followers, his servants, his children, will join him there. Either you are a child of God by being born again through faith in Christ, or you are yet in sin and a follower of the devil.

If you belong to the devil, is it because of the fall of man and the depravity that was brought into the human race, or because of your own choice? For man has only to choose to be a child of God. Jesus said, ". . . him that cometh to me I will in no wise cast out" (John 6:37). None will be turned away that will come to Him in faith.

Freedom is a very precious thing to us all—and we

will argue that until we are exhausted. But if you follow the freedom of man to its logical end, you have to recognize that if a man has freedom in this life, he has freedom also about the life to come. If a man has the freedom to choose the thing he wishes to do, the associates that he has, the things that he wants, the God that he serves in this life, you can be sure that he has also the ultimate choice about where he wishes to spend eternity.

Speaking for God, centuries ago, Moses said, "I have set before you life and death, blessing and cursing: therefore choose life, that both thou and thy seed may live" (Deuteronomy 30:19).

If you are not now a child of God, it is because you have willfully and decisively turned away from God with some excuse. Sinners, having persistently separated themselves from God, banish themselves from His presence and abandon themselves to reap the full harvest of their own evil character and of their rejection of Christ's provision for their sin.

Now you will find many who wish to argue about hell. Let me tenderly leave with you the authority of the Scriptures. In the New Testament, there are many verses that have reference to the place called hell. (This English word is used to translate two different Greek words, *hades* and *gehenna*.) Did not Jesus Himself speak often of hell? Not because He wanted you to go there, but because He was warning you against it.

Jesus was greatly concerned over the destinies of men; the contemplation of the sinner's doom caused His tears. Hear the sob of unwanted love in His plea,

"O Jerusalem, Jerusalem . . . how often would I have gathered thy children together, even as a hen gathereth her chickens under her wings, and ye would not!" (Matthew 23:37).

No preacher can speak about heaven without joy, and no preacher should speak of hell without a sob. That is why, perhaps, we do not speak of it as much as we ought. Yet it is better that men should discover hell from a pulpit than that they should face it unwarned in eternity. I am not happy that hell is there, but it is.

Some people try to explain hell away by saying that it is only in this life and of one's own doing. But we must face the Bible; we must acknowledge the authority of the Scriptures. How can you deny words that came from the lips of Jesus?

In order to go to hell, you literally have to climb over the roadblocks of God. He has done everything within His sovereignty to rescue you. And God is absolutely unlimited except where you have free will, in the space where you limit Him by locking your heart, your life, and saying, "You shall not enter." If you do this, is it not fair for the love of God to say, "Then you cannot enter My kingdom!"

If you were to remove the air from a room, you would have a place where no man could survive. If you remove the presence of God from a man, you have hell— eternal death, no life at all. Hell is what remains after the love of God has been removed. W. T. Conner has written, "A man with sin in his heart could not be happy anywhere in God's universe; he would convert any paradise into a hell. Character is more than environment."

There is no man in hell or on the road to hell or who will go to hell who does not come to that place simply by his own willful, sinful desires and rebellion against God. Somewhere in life you will have to recognize the invitation that comes from the Lord God of Heaven.

The pagans believed that a man was possessed either by a god or by a devil. We must realize that either we ask Christ to enter our life and reign eternally, or we sell ourselves to the devil for temporary privileges. And if you turn God away, then you are turning down the opportunity to go to heaven. There is no other alternative except hell—that is where you have chosen to reside.

Hell is a picture of horrible realization. Hell is a state of merited condemnation. Hell is a void of rejected revelation. But this is not adequate as a description, because hell is more than a picture, it is a place. If heaven is a place of complete happiness for the righteous, then there must be a hell somewhere for those who are separated from God's presence.

A Place of Suffering

From the words of Jesus, we know that hell is *a place of suffering*. You may believe that the passage in Luke 16 is a parable. There are many symbols here, but a symbol is only an instrument to facilitate the expression of what would otherwise be impossible to understand. Nevertheless, the Bible says the man "being in torments"—the plural of the word was scarcely enough to describe the agonies of its physical and mental anguish.

I have heard people say with a sob that sickness is hell, depression is hell, loneliness is hell, divorce is hell, sin is hell, war is hell, disease is hell, alcohol is hell, drugs are hell. All these are true to a degree, but they are the hell of your own design. We are not speaking now of the hell you are making of this life. We are speaking of the eternal and spiritual, not of the material at all.

There are hellish things in life. But when life is over and death comes, the unsaved enter into the second death, which is referred to as hell. It is a multiplied and magnified version of life's worst moments.

The Christian dies only one time: that is, he dies in the flesh. The individual who is not a Christian dies twice. There is a death of flesh and then there is spiritual death—hell. Being limited by our physical senses, we can no more describe hell exactly than we can describe heaven.

If we believe that heaven will be experienced by the saints in a glorious body, then when we leave this body of flesh, hell will dress its prisoners according to its hideous surroundings. Jonathan Edwards said, "If you put your finger over a candle and hold it one inch above the flame, could you hold it one minute? And what about hell—all your body, forever?" We may be in a different body in hell than the one we have here, but that doesn't change the picture of suffering and torment.

As we pass a hospital, can we say that it is only a place of healing, and not a place of suffering? Sometimes in life we suffer with a redemptive quality. You suffer for a little while; you endure pain for the night, but the morning comes. You suffer that you may be well. It seems worth the price to go through suffering that health may return.

Unlike a hospital, hell has no healing or redemptive value. It goes on, not to what would be a blessed annihilation, but with horrible duration. The man there was in torments and cried out, "Have mercy on me; cool my tongue! I am tormented in this place."

Something of the nature of hell might be seen in the drastic change in the rich man. Evidently he rejoiced in the sight of Lazarus, whom all his life he seems to have despised. The man who lacked compassion to pity a beggar became concerned for his brothers. Only extreme torment could produce such belated realizations.

A Place of Separation

The text tells us of a second great tragedy that afflicts the inhabitants of hell: It is *a place of separation*. Just as the finest feature of heaven is the fellowship we have with God, the worst feature of hell will be separation from the presence of God.

"Depart from me," is the command that was spoken by Christ in several places in the New Testament. As Judge of all the earth, He will have cause to repeat it to all those who have rejected Him. Therefore, is not any direction away from God hell?

". . . between us and you there is a great gulf fixed," Jesus quoted Father Abraham in His parable, "so that they which would pass from hence to you cannot; neither can they pass to us, that would come from thence" (Luke 16:26). There was an impassible barrier between the formerly rich man and all the possibilities and personalities of life.

Notice the man's realization that it was impossible for him to leave hell. He had to request Lazarus as an emissary. "Send Lazarus," was his request—first, to wet his tongue, then to go to his brothers. Unfortunately, it was not only impossible for him to go himself, it was also impossible to send a representative, so horribly out of touch with all life was he.

In Revelation 20:14 the Bible speaks of a *second death.* Visualize for a moment the separation of the first death. At a funeral, the loved ones mourn deeply. Then realize they will have no more fellowship, conversation, human touch—no love can pass between them and the departed one. At this time even saints must speak of "the distant shore," for they endure a temporary separation. Yet believers die once, to die no more.

When you accept the fact that you are a sinner and give your life to Jesus Christ as your personal Saviour, crowning Him Lord of your life, then death and hell have no dominion over you.

However, that individual who has rejected Jesus Christ, ignored God, gone another way, chosen the associations of this world against the things of God, has made a willful choice. Imagine, then, the separation of the second death, which will affect only the lost. This separation is not only from loved ones, but from the loving One, God Almighty. It is not just for a time, but for eternity.

If you are this day separated from God, you are making wider the gulf that will one day be fixed so that you can never cross back to life and beauty. Jesus said there is a great gulf fixed: Those from heaven cannot pass to hell. Those in hell, though they wish to escape, have nowhere to go, for there is a vastness of God that engulfs even the confirmed sinner. Because God is everywhere, the sinner can only be *nowhere.*

A Place of Sorrow

Decision during this life determines eternal destiny. Jesus said that there is a great gulf fixed and no man can pass over it. Those in that dismal *place of sorrow* are chained to their position of choice.

Another one of the great sorrows of hell would be separation from our loved ones. But the greatest agony of hell is the absence of God. The only time Jesus wept from the cross was from that pain of separation: "My God, my God, why hast thou absented thyself from me?" (*See* Mark 15:34.)

Could there be anything worse than feeling that God is not near, that He cannot come closer? Yet you have gone through life as through a series of doors, closing them as fast as you can and locking every one of them between you and God. If you play hide-and-seek with God, then you will find no way out. The absence of God is the greatest agony of hell!

Hell's first sorrow is over what has happened. After the rich man requested water from Lazarus, Abraham reminded him, "Son, remember that thou in thy lifetime receivedst thy good things, and likewise Lazarus evil things: but now he is comforted, and thou art tormented" (Luke 16:25).

Hell is, therefore, a place of turned tables. Those who

in this world sought pleasures and shunned God are denied both pleasures and God. Those who were denied pleasures here and sought God for comfort will find pleasures and comfort with God in the Hereafter. In hell, some familiar words of the Lord's Sermon on the Mount will come to mind with great pain: "But seek ye first the kingdom of God, and his righteousness; and all these things shall be added unto you" (Matthew 6:33).

Hell will be full of sorrow for what must yet happen. The rich man knew that as surely as this had been the destiny of his life, it was the destiny for his brothers, as well. When he realized that there was no way out for him, he began to be concerned about those that were still living on earth.

"Father Abraham," he said, "I pray thee, therefore . . . that thou wouldest send him to my father's house (For I have five brethren), that he may testify unto them, lest they also come into this place of torment." (*See* Luke 16:27, 28.) How he wished they could be warned so that they could avoid his suffering!

Unfortunately, hell can hold only wasted concern. Those who in this lifetime passed up the opportunity to be concerned and compassionate regarding the spiritual destiny of loved ones will in hell be eternally sorrowful.

What an indictment for those parents who wickedly neglect the spiritual destinies of their children! What ruin for those whose examples led others to perdition! In this instance, five men, who were following the footsteps of their wealthy older brother, would ultimately plunge into hell. If you do not care for yourself, think about others. Hell holds eternal regret and sorrow.

One of the greatest sorrows of all will be over what might have happened. You will recall that you didn't *have* to be there. Your mind could dwell on all the opportunities for heaven that you ignored. Evil memory will be long in that night of hell. All you can do is remember—you cannot do anything about it. Have you ever tried to sleep when all you seemed to be able to do was remember? Unless you can escape those memories, the sleep which evades you in the night seems to stretch to eternity. In hell, you will have to keep on remembering! That will be one of the sorrows of hell.

If we know God, and His glory and His majesty, we ought to do more about warning people against going to the place the Bible calls hell. God made the earth and He made it perfect. Then the devil came and changed the course of God's creation. Now there is nothing perfect about this world in which we live.

In the beginning, God said, "It is good," but now we see all across our world the handprints of the devil. If we could really imagine that perfect world God created, we could see the incredible contrast of our present chaos. God was the Great Designer, but what He made and called good, the devil has wrecked until it is becoming unlivable. Why? Because man chose to follow the devil and let him have control. Why then would you want to live in a hell shaped by the devil?

We have been promised a perfect place, a heaven of escape which has been designed by God for us. "I go to prepare a place for you," Jesus said (John 14:2). And God is getting that place ready now. Why choose the worst when you can have the best?

There was never a baby born that God intended to go to hell. "Come now, and let us reason together . . ." the Bible exhorts (Isaiah 1:18). When ultimately a man is condemned, the reasoning always points to choice, and it's your choice. It depends on whether or not you want to choose what God has prepared for you. May the authority of God's Word reason with you. Why would you choose death when you might have life?

I am told that early on the evening the *Titanic* sank, the orchestra was playing festively, "There'll Be a Hot Time in the Old Town Tonight." But when news spread that the unsinkable ship was going down, and the water was nearly up to the decks, the last tune that orchestra played was, "Nearer, My God, to Thee." What changed the celebration? Was it not the proximity of tragic reality?

"When the Son of man shall come in his glory," the Lord foretold, "and all the holy angels with him, then shall he sit upon the throne of his glory . . ." (Matthew 25:31). He who died for us will be our Judge. If we reject Him, He must reject us. "Then shall he say also unto them on the left hand, Depart from me, ye cursed, into everlasting fire . . . . but the righteous into life eternal" (Matthew 25:41, 46).

He is not yet Judge, He is still the beseeching Saviour. "Behold, I stand at the door, and knock," He pleads. "If any man will open the door, I will come in and sup with him, and he with me." (*See* Revelation 3:20.) Are you going to exchange that fellowship with God for an eternity in hell?

7—SECOND COMING:
Ready for the Returning Redeemer

Jesus said: *Therefore be ye also ready.''*
Matthew 24:44

Not since the first century has the doctrine of the Second Coming of Christ been so much talked about as in our day. It is actually popular and commercialized. A sign of our times is the sight of young people with their hands pointed to the skies, saying, "Jesus is the One Way," and "Jesus is coming back!"

On bumper stickers we read: GUESS WHO IS COMING AGAIN? Or the warning: IN CASE OF THE RAPTURE, THIS CAR WILL BE DRIVERLESS.

We are caught up in predictions of future events. Scientists predict worldwide famine. Economists predict continued inflation and depression. Everybody is wondering why somebody didn't predict the energy crisis and the ecology problems. Never has the craze of Ouija boards, crystal balls, fortune-telling cards, and horoscopes been so popular. A major obsession of our hour is the search for the mysterious and unknown.

Perhaps one reason we are so preoccupied with the future is that we despair of the present. Accompanied with much hand wringing, we hear, "What is the world coming to?" on the lips of both old and young. Neither do Christians know what the world is coming to, but we do know *Who* is coming to the world—the King of Kings is coming!

Without doubt, the most important question in all of life is, "Do you know Jesus Christ in personal salvation?" Then the next most important question is, "Are you ready for the return of the Redeemer?"

Anyone who reads the Bible is confronted with the fact that one day God proposes to end history as we know it. And its end will be signaled by the Second Coming, the return of God's own Son. The Bible starts out: "In the beginning God . . ." (Genesis 1:1) and it closes with, "He which testifieth these things saith, Surely I come quickly. Amen. Even so, come, Lord Jesus" (Revelation 22:20).

Traditionally and historically, certain essential statements make up the Christian confession: "I believe that Jesus Christ is the Son of God . . . born of a virgin . . . died on the cross . . . arose from the grave and ascended into heaven, where He sits on the right hand of God the Father Almighty . . . and is coming again." Remove any of these essential things and you have made a lesser Christ.

In 1919, Woodrow Wilson said in a Senate speech that the League of Nations was the only hope of mankind. He was pleading for its ratification. I have seen the building they erected in Switzerland to house that hope, but the League of Nations was never ratified by the Senate of the United States. It was not considered the hope of America.

Christ was then and is now the only hope of the world—of this world and of the next world. Gladly we should await His return.

What will be the signs of Christ's coming? Let us look back and examine His first coming. His entry was quiet. His birth was announced to only a few and only a few recognized Him as God. But the second time, He will appear in glory rather than in humiliation. He will return with a shout, and everyone from the four corners of the earth will see and know Him.

"And then shall they see the Son of man coming in the clouds with great power and glory," Jesus told his disciples (Mark 13:26).

The first time He came to redeem; the second time He will come to reign. The first time He came to die; the second time He will bring resurrection to the bodies of millions. The first time He was born King of the Jews; the second time He will be revealed as the King of kings. The first time He came in poverty; but He shall return in power. The first time He was given a crown of thorns; but the second time He will wear a crown of glory.

The Second Coming of our Lord is an essential doctrine of the Bible. It has been said by some that this event is as important to our redemption as His first coming. God's Word tells us that His return is sure and that it will be secret and sudden.

Sure

His return is as *sure* as the promises of God. "Heaven and earth shall pass away, but my words shall not pass away," Jesus said (Matthew 24:35). He has never broken a promise He made to us, and He said, "I will come

again" (John 14:3). In the New Testament, His Second
Coming is mentioned 318 times.

There are some things we cannot know about the
Second Coming, but there are some sure things we are
told concerning His return.

During the dark days of World War II, when General
Douglas MacArthur had to withdraw from the Philip-
pines, he declared, "I shall return!" The people hoped
in his promise because that was all the hope they had.
They believed in his integrity and, providentially, he
was able to keep his promise. But because the general
was only human, his promise was in some doubt, no
matter how firm his intention.

Never have the promises of God been in doubt to any
man, in any generation, at any season. Christ's coming
is our hope and our surety. Near the end of His ministry, Jesus Christ gave the greatest promises of His return. Knowing that His trial and crucifixion would stun
them almost out of their faith, He purposely dwelt on
those truths that would realize their expectations of
Him in a far more glorious way than they had ever yet
dreamed.

What you have locked up in the bank cannot provide
you with such security; it is not adequate for all the
possibilities of the future. The coming again of Jesus is
the Christian's hope and confidence. We must watch
for the signs of His coming. We must listen for the
sounds of His coming. We must anticipate the sight of
His glory; we must live our lives in hope.

"Now learn a parable of the fig tree," Jesus said to
His disciples. "When her branch is yet tender, and put-
teth forth leaves, ye know that summer is near: So ye in

like manner, when ye shall see these things come to pass, know that it [the Lord's coming] is nigh, even at the doors" (Mark 13:28, 29). There are times when we scarcely notice how one season changes into another. But as sure as the signs of the seasons—and even more than that—His coming is as sure as His words.

Secret

The coming of Jesus Christ will be *secret,* as secret as the flood waters swirling and swelling in the night.

Most of the world lives as though they feel they will get some kind of second chance. Or that they will have advance notice, that someone will come and say, "Get ready, Jesus is coming!" That is exactly what every preacher is doing when he preaches on the Second Coming. I am an advance man for the coming again of Jesus Christ!

Even most Christians live as though we don't expect Him to come. We live as though we don't expect death to come. We live as though we don't expect Jesus Christ to interfere with our plans.

Jesus said His coming will be as God Himself decides, and we will have no say in the matter. "But of that day and hour knoweth no man, no, not the angels of heaven, but my Father only" (Matthew 24:36).

An old-time preacher once said that when somebody starts predicting to you that they know exactly the time Jesus is coming back, you'd better lock your chicken house. Maybe he was right, because Jesus said His coming would be "as a thief in the night." The angels do not know—only God the Father knows. He has not imparted it to us—not to one single person. Not even Jesus Himself knew, when He was on earth.

When Noah preached that the flood was coming, people didn't listen to him. Noah went out and built the ark, waking up a few and disturbing their rest as he hammered away. At the same time, he and his sons preached the coming judgment: God was going to send a flood because of human wickedness. But the others didn't believe them. Noah went on hammering. The others went on sleeping. The flood came upon them suddenly—they were not expecting it.

Jesus summed up and applied this event:

> But as the days of Noe were, so shall also the coming of the Son of man be. For as in the days that were before the flood they . . . knew not until the flood came, and took them all away; so shall also the coming of the Son of man be.
>
> Matthew 24:37–39

Just that sudden will be the coming again of Jesus Christ.

Each day's sunset is a silent and secret thing. We know it is coming; we may even anticipate it down to the minute. But sunset falls as silently over the earth as a shadow across the grass. So will the Second Coming occur in just the tick of the clock, just as the sun hides itself, just as the moon comes up. Just as suddenly as that; just as certainly as that. Just as sure as that will be the secret coming of the Lord Jesus Christ.

Imagine the secrecy of God's election: "Then shall two be in the field; the one shall be taken, and the other left. Two women shall be grinding at the mill; the one shall be taken, and the other left" (Matthew 24: 40, 41).

Jesus said that we must watch and wait. Bear in mind the emphasis is upon the watching and not upon the waiting, because watching is an activity. Waiting is passive. Watching is exciting; waiting is boring.

Have you watched for a train or a plane? Waiting, you may nearly go to sleep. But there is a roar, a rush, and you begin to be alert with anticipation. Just as surely as the blast of the whistle when the train approaches the depot, the trumpet will sound and the King will return.

Sudden

No one knows the exact moment when the Lord will return. His coming will be *sudden.* "Watch, therefore," Jesus said, "for ye know neither the day nor the hour wherein the Son of man cometh" (Matthew 25:13). We need to be ready for the returning Redeemer. He could come in the quietness of the night. He could come while we are sleeping. Watch, therefore! It will be as silent as moonrise, as sudden as a thief.

You may know the statistics on how many homes are robbed annually. You may be able to estimate how many in your town will be robbed this year, but you do not know when your home might be the one. If you did, you would be better prepared; you would set up a watch.

"But know this," Jesus said, "that if the goodman of the house had known in what watch the thief would come, he would have watched, and would not have suffered his house to be broken up." What has this to do with us? "Therefore be ye also ready: for in such an hour as ye think not the Son of man cometh" (Matthew 24:43, 44).

Can you remember when you were in school? Sometimes the teacher left the room, telling you to behave while she was gone. She told you she was coming back shortly. But just as soon as she got out the door and her shadow left the hall, you took the chance; you began to talk, to play, to fight.

Suddenly an awkward silence. It seemed you were the only one caught talking—your mouth open, but no words coming out. The teacher stood in the door. When you were prepared for her return, you didn't have to be afraid. But if you were unprepared, doing something undisciplined, the teacher's return was sure to seem quite sudden.

Jesus gave another parable to illustrate the suddenness of His return.

> Who then is a faithful and wise servant, whom his lord hath made ruler over his household, to give them meat in due season? Blessed is that servant whom his lord when he cometh shall find so doing. Verily I say unto you, That he shall make him ruler over all his goods.
>
> [On the other hand] if that evil servant shall say in his heart, My lord delayeth his coming; And shall begin to smite his fellowservants, and to eat and drink with the drunken; The lord of

that servant shall come in a day when he looketh
not for him, and in an hour that he is not aware
of.

Matthew 24:45–50

Jesus was saying, "Blessed is that servant who knows
not when his master will return, yet he is busy with his
duties." Such a servant is faithful and wise. Can Jesus
say "blessed" concerning you?

The Jehovah's Witnesses, based on the predictions of
Charles Russell that Jesus would come in 1914, say that
He has already returned, and this group has developed
some following. But, according to what the Bible de-
scribes, He has not come yet. I choose to believe the
Bible.

Many men have tried to predict the exact time, the
exact year, the exact moment of the coming again of the
Lord. There was a man by the name of William Miller
who predicted that Jesus would come at a certain hour
in the year 1843. Brigham Young brought hope to a vast
number of his followers who believed his announcement that Jesus would come in the year 1891.

One early morning hour in the city of Los Angeles, a
well-meaning but ill-advised preacher got a group of
people out on the housetops, wrapped in white sheets.
They were hoping to be the first to see Jesus' return;
they were going to be there, ready when He came. I do
not speak unkindly, but they were ready for only one
thing—what some of them got for their trouble—
pneumonia. They thought they knew the exact moment when the clouds would part and Jesus would

come—but they were wrong.

Jesus' return will be sudden and at God's own time, not any time of our guessing.

In the first century, some Thessalonian Christians quit work to wait for Christ's return. They stopped everything they were doing and waited passively. In the language of our day, they became religious "bums." They thought that was how to get ready for the returning Redeemer. Paul reprimanded them: "For even when we were with you, this we commanded you, that if any would not work, neither should he eat. For we hear that there are some which walk among you disorderly, working not at all, but are busybodies" (2 Thessalonians 3:10, 11).

The way you get ready for the returning Redeemer is to get other people ready. The apostle Paul reproached those Christians in Thessalonica for just sitting around, just waiting, not watching. Watching is an active process. We must be ready and busy preparing all the time.

First, we must be righteous: "And every man that hath this hope in him purifieth himself, even as he is pure" (1 John 3:3). Our watching should include the effort of keeping on, of being faithful and doing good as God has put in our hearts.

We must also evangelize: "And this gospel of the kingdom shall be preached in all the world for a witness unto all nations; and then shall the end come" (Matthew 24:14). Jesus said He would not come until the Gospel is preached to the four corners of the earth. To get ready for His coming again, we must preach the Gospel, not only to the heathen across the sea but to the heathen in our city and on our street. We must evangelize a lost world.

We must watch with expectancy, with anticipation. "Henceforth there is laid up for me a crown of righteousness, which the Lord, the righteous judge, shall give me at that day: and not to me only, but unto all them also that love his appearing" (2 Timothy 4:8). Not everyone loves His appearing. Some who believe He is coming take a fearful attitude about it. They feel that it is an unwelcome, disturbing thing.

Rather, it should be like the first exciting chord on the organ when the wedding march begins and the bride's party starts down the aisle. There is that kind of anticipation about the return of the blessed Redeemer. He said we are to *love* His coming. Do you love His coming?

Would you say, "Even so, come, Lord Jesus"? (Revelation 22:20.)

Or would you say, "I wish He would wait awhile; there are some things I haven't gotten right. I want to be one of those taken, and not one of those left." Have you prepared for it? He said, "Whosoever therefore shall confess me before men, him will I confess also before my Father which is in heaven" (Matthew 10:32).

Sometime, back there, you may have given your heart to Christ, and really intended to follow Him as an obedient Christian. But the truth of the matter is, you haven't done that and you don't love His coming.

Are you serving Him? Are things up-to-date? Have you gotten things out of your heart, out of your system, out of your mind? Have you prepared your heart and soul for His coming as you would your house for special guests?

The apostle Paul said the grace of God teaches us that ". . . denying ungodliness and worldly lusts, we should live soberly, righteously, and godly, in this present world; Looking for that blessed hope, and the glorious appearing of the great God and our Saviour Jesus Christ" (Titus 2:12, 13).

A French chemist predicted many years ago that "within a hundred years of physical and chemical science, man will know what the atom is. It is my belief when science reaches this stage, God will come down to earth with His big ring of keys and say to humanity, 'Gentlemen, it's closing time!' "

One of these days the Keeper of History will ring down the curtain. It will be swift, it will be sure, it will be sudden, and it will be secret. But He is coming.

How long must we wait? Many signs of His coming seem to be fulfilled in our time. Are you ready?

8—JUDGMENT:
Case Closed, No Appeal!

Jesus said: *"For the Father . . . hath committed all judgment unto the Son."*

John 5:22

Judgment and justice are two very real concerns of our day. The media are full of hearings, trials, and sentences. In recent decades, we have grown accustomed to the sounds and sights of judgment. In the 1940s there was the Nuremberg trial, in the 1950s the Rosenberg trial, in the 1960s numerous assassinations before our very eyes. In the 1970s we had Watergate!

The sound of the gavel, the clang of the jail door, the despair of prisoners, are signs of judgments assessed.

Though we are familiar with judgments, we often forget too quickly and easily our personal responsibilities for righteousness. Much personal failure is clinically excused by apologetic psychologists. Others insist that environment rather than choice affects destinies. The prevalent motto of many is: "It's all right as long as it hurts no one." But it does. All over the world, people act as though there were no consequences. "It's all right," is the tune we dance to. Dare we examine ourselves and our world?

Children commit wrongs without fear of discipline.

Drug users steal to support their habits. Men exploit sex, bringing heartbreak and disease. Violence stalks the streets and the witnesses refuse to get involved. Criminals often escape through loopholes of the law. Some people feel that the rights of honest people have disappeared.

People today are basically the same as in Jeremiah's time: "Why then is this people of Jerusalem slidden back by a perpetual backsliding? they hold fast deceit, they refuse to return. I hearkened and heard, but they spake not aright: no man repented him of his wickedness, saying, What have I done? . . ." (Jeremiah 8:5, 6).

Could it be that we also have ignored consequences? We have refused to consider the judgment, or any day of reckoning, or any answer that we might be required to give.

In the Greater Greensboro Open Golf Tournament of 1972, Gary Player was in line for first place and a pot of $40,000. However, he was denied the prize due to a technicality: He did not sign his scorecard as the game progressed.

When asked how he felt about not receiving the prize, Mr. Player replied, "I read the rules before I entered. I did not observe the rules of the game. Therefore, I must accept the consequences."

Life on the sidewalk is no different from that on the golf course. The Bible gives us the rules of the game of life. If we break the rules, we have to accept the consequences.

There are many rules of life. Some are set by man, and they may be just or unjust. If they are laws, they are laws, whether wise or unwise. But if they are the ultimate laws of God, then they cannot be declared unjust by any man.

For the judgment of all men by a holy and righteous God there is an appointed day, an awaited Judge, and an appropriate verdict.

The Appointed Day

Whether we like it or not, *the appointed Day* of Judgment will come. The Bible says, "And as it is appointed unto men once to die, but after this the judgment" (Hebrews 9:27).

Jesus spoke of it often: "Verily, verily, I say unto you, The hour is coming, and now is, when the dead shall hear the voice of the Son of God: and they that hear shall live" (John 5:25).

Ray Summers has said, "If God is righteous, He must exercise mercy on the obedient and mete out punishment to the disobedient." Judgment is sure. Men dare not run away from its reality.

Jesus told a parable about a rich fool who said to himself, without any regard for the Hereafter, "I shall tear down *my* barns, *I* will build bigger barns." (*See* Luke 12:18.) He went on with the *I*'s, without taking into consideration that one day God would demand an accounting of his own life, as he demanded an accounting of those who worked for him.

"But God said unto him, Thou fool, this night thy soul shall be required of thee: then whose shall those things be, which thou hast provided?" (Luke 12:20). The Day of Judgment is coming. The day of death may come even sooner.

A rich potentate in Asia gave to his court jester a beautiful scepter, because he thought him a great comic, a great fool, a great entertainer. "Keep this until you find a greater fool than you are," said the king, thinking that was the best compliment he could pay the man.

Days passed and life went on. The jester was called in because the ruler was dying. As he came into the presence of his king, that monarch greeted him, "Do you know I am going on a long journey?"

"Where are you going?" the court jester questioned.

"Into the dark, I do not know where."

"Have you prepared for the journey?"

"Alas, I have made no preparation. I do not know where I go, but it will be forever."

The court jester turned and apologetically—but wishing to arouse in his king a sense of reckoning—laid in the hands of his master the scepter. "Sir," he said, "I respectfully return this to you, because you are a bigger fool than I am, if you will make a journey without any preparation."

In the journey of life, in the journey toward a time of accounting, have you made preparation?

It is said that on one occasion W. C. Fields was seen thumbing through the Bible on a Hollywood set. Several people noticed, especially because they felt reading the Bible was out of character for him. Finally someone got up courage to speak. "Why are you reading the Bible?"

"I am trying to find loopholes," said Mr. Fields. "I am hunting for any loopholes there might be." But he found none.

Many people go through life looking for loopholes, giving excuses, and saying, "The reason I have never made a decision is because there are others whose decisions are meaningless. Look at the hypocrites in the church!" People who say this are looking for loopholes.

Loopholes will do you no good at the Judgment, because there are none in God's Word. "How shall we escape," asked the writer of Hebrews 2:3, "if we neglect so great salvation . . . ."

The Awaited Judge

There is not only the appointed day, there is *the awaited Judge.*

Some think of the Saviour only as "Gentle Jesus, meek and mild." We teach the children this, and they *should* be taught of His mercy, His gentleness, His love.

But Paul said, ". . . when I became a man, I put away childish things" (1 Corinthians 13:11). There is such a thing as an age of responsibility, a coming day of accountability. We should be looking for Jesus to come again as King, expecting the One who is not only meek and mild, but who can be terrible in the Day of Judgment. That baby who lay in the manger grew up and became the crucified One on Calvary, the resurrected One from the grave, the ascended One into heaven, the returning One someday. In the end, He will be Judge of all.

"For the Father judgeth no man," Jesus said, "but hath committed all judgment unto the Son" (John 5:22). "In this terminus of a future and final catastrophe, Jesus himself is the judge," said Dr. Herbert Lockyer, "and no thought in his teaching is more frequent than this. Thus a marked feature in his solemn words about this concluding judgment is his phrase, 'That day!' "

The apostle Jude later commented, "Behold, the Lord cometh with ten thousands of his saints, To execute judgment upon all, and to convince all that are ungodly among them of all their ungodly deeds which they have ungodly committed." (*See* Jude 14, 15.) Not only is Jesus Christ the Saviour of the world, He is King of kings and will be Judge of all men.

A young criminal lawyer named Warren Chandler pled the case of a young man on trial for his life—and won the verdict. As the man went free, Mr. Chandler, a Christian gentleman, said to his client, "Now you have another chance in society. Give your life to God. Live right and do right."

Years passed. The young lawyer became a judge, and the young criminal went on with a life of crime. Later, he was brought to trial before Judge Chandler.

The jury brought in its verdict. Before the judge read it, he addressed the accused man. "I recall from my records that many years ago you stood beside me and I pled your case and you were acquitted. But today you stand before me as your judge. It is my responsibility by the laws of this state to assess upon you the death penalty. You will die in the electric chair."

That situation between Judge Chandler and his former client is paralleled in every life. A man who has encountered Jesus Christ as his Advocate and turned away from Him, one day will find Christ no longer standing beside him and pleading his case to God the

Father. At present, Christ invites, "Behold, I stand at the door, and knock: if any man hear my voice, and open the door, I will come in to him, and will sup with him, and he with me" (Revelation 3:20).

One day Christ will be the Judge, and if He is not your Saviour, He will judge your life and find it wanting. The day of salvation will be over and the Day of Judgment will be upon you. We await the Judge of all the earth.

It was reported that the agnostic lawyer and orator, Bob Ingersoll, in a public speech was ridiculing all things religious and making fun of anything that was right. Finally a drunken hearer stood up and said before the thousands assembled, "Bob, make it good! A lot of us are depending on you!"

You are going to have to decide whether you will be the follower of Bob Ingersoll, choosing his philosophy in your heart, or whether you will turn to Jesus Christ and let Him be your Saviour. Because one day He will be your Judge. He is the awaited Judge.

The Appropriate Verdict

He can be your Saviour. But if you turn down the loving invitation of the Lord Jesus, then there is *the appropriate verdict,* an inevitable verdict. Novels, movies, TV series, life itself, depict injustices of man to man. They illustrate very dramatically the wrongs that have been committed. These stories point out human selfishness and human error.

Even the courts of men have had to reverse themselves occasionally. And with good reason, because the courts of earth can do wrong, because they act on partial knowledge and circumstantial evidence.

When you stand before the Awaited Judge, you can claim no extenuating circumstances. There will be no reasonable doubt. There will be no half-way evidence. All things will be open before Him. ". . . there is nothing covered," Jesus said, "that shall not be revealed; and hid, that shall not be known" (Matthew 10:26).

The Judgment of God will be sure and swift—also pure, and just, and definite. Then the case will be closed. There can be no appeal, because there is no higher court. God's judgments are always just and final. The laws of God are simple. There are only two types of cases: only one of two sentences will He give.

What things distinguish between those who receive the different sentences? "He that believeth on him is not condemned: but he that believeth not is condemned already, [*Why?*] because he hath not believed in the name of the only begotten Son of God" (John 3:18). So the only reason a man is saved or unsaved is his belief or unbelief.

The only difference that marks the saint of God, who can claim the privileges of heaven in that day, is that he can say, "Not by works of righteousness which we have done, but according to his mercy he saved us . . ." (Titus 3:5). Because a person has believed and exercised faith and trusted Jesus, he is a Christian.

"He that heareth my word," Jesus said, "and believeth on him that sent me, hath everlasting life, and shall not come into condemnation; but is passed from death unto life" (John 5:24).

If you have not believed, however, because of your unbelief the Bible pronounces you unsaved here and now. You do not have to wait until you get to the Judgment—already you are lost. You will not have to wait until then, for then it will be too late to make the decision. Already he is condemned who "hath not believed in the name of the only begotten Son of God."

What is the degree of punishment? Is it fair? The Bible says, "Judge not, that ye be not judged" (Matthew 7:1). If you turn away from Jesus, then you are judging Him unworthy of your trust, your affection, your life. You are accounting Jesus a liar. You are turning Him down.

Therefore, if you have the right to turn Him down—and you do—you must recognize that in the Day of Judgment, the Judge has the right to hand down a verdict of guilty. You are indeed guilty—guilty of rejecting Christ, who is the Son of God and the Judge of the earth.

To that one who has not believed, He will say, "I never knew you: depart from me, ye that work iniquity" (Matthew 7:23). That is the appropriate verdict.

To the one who has believed, He will say, "Well done, thou good and faithful servant: thou hast been faithful over a few things, I will make thee ruler over many things: enter thou into the joy of thy lord" (Matthew 25:21).

Out in the western United States, in Zion National Park, there is a great white rock that stands several thousand feet high. When the early settlers saw it for the first time, they named it The Great White Throne. That name was passed on from one wagon train to another, from one settler to another, until it is still called that today.

God has placed throughout His revelation, not only geographically but biographically, the signposts of destiny in every life. God has placed before you the revelation of His will. God has asked you not to deviate from His path.

A popular entertainer has made America laugh with him when he says, flippantly and often, "Here come de judge!"

But it will be no laughing matter when the Judge of all the earth comes. We will stand before Him and be judged by the One we have been judging. For we are now judging Jesus as worthy of our life or unworthy of our life. And because He died for us and is willing to save us now, and because He is sure and steadfast, He will elect you if you will elect Him.

Here comes the Judge! The Judgment of God begins here and now. One day the case will be closed. There will be no more appeals from the pulpit to your heart. There will be no appealing the sentence, either. You will be sentenced to exile from everything that is God and that is good, forever.

There can be no place in God's Kingdom for the rebellious and those who have iniquity in their hearts.

The supreme Judge says, "Case closed! No appeal!"

9—TREASURE:
Double Dividends

> Jesus said: *"But lay up for yourselves treasures in heaven."*
>
> Matthew 6:20

You cannot be a slave to two things at once, Jesus said. You cannot be a good servant of God and at the same time be a slave to riches. Christians should not become addicted to money. God intends for us to have mastery over it.

It may sound strange to say so, but Jesus is interested in what money can do for you. Listen to Him: "Lay not up for yourselves treasures upon earth, where moth and rust doth corrupt, and where thieves break through and steal: But lay up for yourselves treasures in heaven . . ." (Matthew 6:19, 20).

In Paul's letter to young Timothy we find the well-known but often misquoted passage about money being the root of all evil. That is not what Paul said. Money itself is nothing more than a piece of metal or paper, a possession with bargaining power, a medium of exchange. This thing in itself is never evil; it is neutral, entirely under the control of those who use it.

What Paul really said was that "the *love* of money is the root of all evil" (1 Timothy 6:10). Be careful, then, that you control the money, rather than letting the money control you. There is a difference between need of money and love of money. The *love* of money, to serve only for what you can get, is indeed a root of every evil.

Greed damages everything it touches. Many marriages fail because of money problems. Bickering over money can damage love in the home. Money cannot be divorced from our domestic relationships; neither can it be divorced from our spiritual life.

Money is not a thing used only in the commerce of the civilization in which we live. It becomes part of a man's motives, a spur to his efforts, basic to his performance, an index of his production. God has commanded us to labor, and in our society money is the most usual fruit of our labor. Surely this cannot be sin! It is not the dollars themselves, but how we use the fruit of our labor, that shows the love of our hearts.

Jesus Christ did not remain silent on financial things. He got to the heart of the matter in a very direct way: "For where your treasure is, there will your heart be also" (Matthew 6:21). Our hearts follow our money. There are not many people who put money into the church when they do not attend church. We have a way of relating to whatever we invest in—part of our love goes there, too.

In the era of materialism in which Christ lived, He said to those people (and to us), "No man can serve two masters: for either he will hate the one, and love the other; or else he will hold to the one, and despise the other. Ye cannot serve God and mammon" (Matthew 6:24). You must make a choice. Which one will be the master of your life?

No better illustration could we find than Jesus' contact with Zacchaeus. This little man evidently had a great love for money; he was willing to sell out his own people; he served Rome at their expense.

But Jesus invited Himself to be the guest of Zacchaeus. Because of the conversation they had in the home that day, and because of what Zacchaeus saw in Jesus, he decided to make Jesus the Master of his life. That settled once and for all his money problem.

Listen to him: "Behold, Lord, the half of my goods I give to the poor; and if I have taken any thing from any man by false accusation, I restore him fourfold" (Luke 19:8).

Who is going to master the house of your heart?

At another time, a young man of wealth and prestige came to Jesus. "Good Master," he asked, "what shall I do that I may inherit eternal life?" (Mark 10:17).

Jesus listed the six commandments pertaining to human relationships and told him to keep them.

"Master, all these have I observed from my youth," the young man replied proudly (v. 20).

Then Jesus said to him, "One thing thou lackest: go thy way, sell whatsoever thou hast, and give to the poor, and thou shalt have treasure in heaven . . ." (v. 21).

The young man turned sorrowfully and "went away grieved." The Way was too hard for him—he loved his money too much.

This is one of the few times in the New Testament we read of a man coming to Jesus enthusiastically, asking Him for something, and going away less happy than when he came. Almost everyone who came to Jesus went away with a song in his heart, a healed body, a great experience of God. But this young man, because he decided not to let God be Master of his life, went away grieved. Because he decided to let money be his master, he forfeited all that God had to offer him.

Most men who are mastered by possessions become soured in disposition. The love of money breeds covetousness, envy, jealousy—and these things damage the spiritual gifts that God gives us. It is not long until we fail to notice anything that God has given, and we lose the gratitude which man must have if he serves God.

The basic problem is not with money itself, but with our attitude toward it. The Master's admonition to deposit our treasures in heaven guides us into the best and wisest course.

Appeal

We have to recognize that treasure—or money, if you please—has a universal *appeal* to every man, no matter what his vocation. To this appeal Jesus addressed Himself. Money so easily becomes far more than a status symbol; it becomes an emotional necessity.

In the search for the truly necessary things of life, we easily lose our sense of priorities and forget what money is for and why we wanted it. We are supposed to use it for the grace of generosity, which blesses both giver and receiver. Instead, unfortunately, we often allow ourselves to become drugged by it.

Jesus faced this deadly combat over material things when Satan tempted Him with the offer of the whole world. "Then saith Jesus unto him, Get thee hence,

Satan: for it is written, Thou shalt worship the Lord thy God, and him only shalt thou serve" (Matthew 4:10). Satan still uses that temptation with any man who commits himself to serve God. Many a man has not lived to his full potential in the service of God because he has lost the battle with greed.

What is success? What is the symbol of true and spiritual success? Money would be high on the list of things that accompany success, but it should not be the only thing. In the Sermon on the Mount, Jesus mentioned that the Kingdom man, the Christian man, the righteous man, the godly man, is the one who is blessed.

"Blessed are they which do hunger and thirst after righteousness: for they shall be filled" (Matthew 5:6). Translated into the language of today: "Happy is that man who does the things God asks him to do!" Success is not being highly rated in financial circles or being among the socially elite or famous and newsworthy. Jesus listed His rules for success and happiness in the Sermon on the Mount.

Jesus is quoted as saying, "It is more blessed to give than to receive" (Acts 20:35). This is often called the best Beatitude, and it is a comparison rather than a contrast.

Under some circumstances, it is very good to receive. If a parent receives a gift of gratitude from a child, it is a wonderful thing. It is a beautiful expression of love; it is a meaningful experience. But if it becomes necessary for the parent to be supported by the child—as far as the parent is concerned, it is a grievous thing. Because there is an underlying rule of life: It is more blessed to

give than to receive. It is even better to be the be-
stower than to be the beneficiary.

It is far better when we have the ability to give—
whether it is material things or spiritual things. But
also I speak in the sense of giving your talents in service
to God.

Why do we so often reject this teaching of Jesus concerning giving? Because it cuts across the grain. Let's
be honest with ourselves. We have to fight our carnal
natures everyday of our lives. You fight it on Sunday;
whether to get up and come to church, and how much
you are going to give to God. You are aware of the
appeal of many interests; you have to decide where you
are going to put your priorities.

Attitude

Knowing the principle, what should be our *attitude*
toward money and its use? Should we just be silent
concerning money? Yet silence is often a dangerous sin.
Phillips Brooks once said that the greatest temptation of
the preacher is to say smooth things rather than true
things. It is easier to say the things that people want to
hear than the things they need to hear.

Jesus did not take a hands-off policy in His attitude
toward money. "And Jesus sat over against the treasury," we read, "and beheld how the people cast
money into the treasury . . ." (Mark 12:41). He was
interested. He watched the great and the near great. He
watched what we would call big and little gifts, although, actually, there are no little gifts. Concerning
the woman who came and offered the least amount that
day, Jesus said to His disciples, "This poor widow hath

cast more in, than all they which have cast into the treasury" (Mark 12:43).

Remember that this woman was a widow who had so little to give that it was an apology. But it was all that she had. Did she dream that what she put into the treasury at that moment would be recorded in God's Word? You never dream that what you give to the church can make a resounding difference. We never dare to think that what we invest in a Sunday school class could change a life which in turn might change the world.

That little widow didn't dream of greatness or fame. She recognized the love of her heart, the gratitude of her soul, and her obligation to God. Because she knew that in everything, she had to depend upon God to take care of her, the emotion of her soul swelled up to the extent that she gave all that she had. Jesus sat and watched and commended her.

God constantly makes divine appraisal of our gifts— the ones that we put on the altar as well as the ones we make in our lives. We must recognize that our attitude toward the gift of our lives inevitably reflects the radiance of our souls. If all that we can see is money, our lives are impoverished.

Henry Ford, when he was a young man just becoming rich, had been impressed with this Scripture that the love of money is the root of all evil. He took two silver dollars and had them put in spectacle frames. Keeping them on his desk, he occasionally took off his glasses and put them on, to keep himself from falling into the pattern of so many other men who could see only money.

If the only treasure that you have is what rattles in your pocket, rather than the love in the recesses of your heart, you are a poverty-stricken person. Money can be either corn or currency, of course. Jesus was talking about treasures, which is far more. The Roman matron of long ago was not far wrong when she brought her two children and said, "These are my jewels." That is, "These are the only things I have that I value. These are the important things that have priority in my life."

Alexander the Great requested that when he died, his coffin should be made with holes, so that his hands might protrude on the outside. He knew that, for all his conquests and power, he would go out of this life empty-handed.

"Lay not up for yourselves treasures on earth," Jesus said. You can't take it with you. Nearly one-sixth of the recorded spoken words of Jesus pertain to attitudes that we should have concerning money. What is the appeal of money in your life?

In a country cemetery, there is a stinging epitaph which reads, "Born a man, died only a merchant. His soul was kicked to death for what he had." Though this may not be on our tombstone, it may be an epitaph by which men remember us. Our attitude toward money brightens or tarnishes everything we do.

Admonition

What was Christ's *admonition?* "Lay not up for yourselves treasures upon earth." Why?

For one thing, here thieves may break in and carry them off. Jesus continued, ". . . where moth and rust doth corrupt, and where thieves break through and steal" (Matthew 6:19).

In the time in which Jesus lived, dwellings were mostly either rock buildings or mud huts. It was very easy for a thief to dig through a wall of mud brick and go into a house. There was no such thing as a bank on every corner.

Those who lived in tents often buried their money. In that desert area, sometimes shifting winds came during the night and all landmarks would be erased that might guide a man back to where he had buried his hoard. He might have laid away his treasure, never to find it again.

If a man put his money into fine garments and tapestries, moths might damage them. Whatever is hoarded, something will corrupt it. It will lose its luster. It will tarnish. It will decay.

During one Christmas season, I remember hearing someone say they were going to town to collect their layaways. Now, layaways are what Jesus was talking about here. One day we will go and collect the treasures we have "put on layaway" with Him. We cannot take them with us, but we can send them on ahead. Whatever is invested in heaven will be what is invested in the lives of other people: a song, a sermon, a lesson, an attendance whereby you speak your attitude toward God and godly things.

It might be a gift you gave. It will be something that you did to enrich the lives of others. Investing in those things, you will never know the good that you do until you come to the end of the way.

In a church bulletin appeared this little warning: "Please do not leave any money in the classrooms because everybody around here is not converted." That is an obvious problem in many congregations. Church buildings may be broken into even during the worship services. Choir rooms have to be secured so that no one can enter and raid the members' purses while they are in the choir loft. Everyone is not converted.

Yet some say that churches try to pick your pocket. No, we are simply trying to prick your heart to a new understanding of what is involved in your attitude toward money. Martin Luther said that every man ought to have two conversions: He ought to be converted in his heart and he ought to be converted in his pocketbook.

God can multiply our gifts where we cannot do more. You may prosper, but you should remember that the things done in partnership with God will prosper much more than anything you can do on your own.

One of the great churches of the East was bought and paid for, and in it one of the world's famous sermons, called "Acres of Diamonds," was preached by Russell Conwell. The story behind that building and sermon began with a child's gift of less than a dollar.

A little girl heard the appeal by the pastor: They needed to build a building, but a lot had to be bought, for which the set price seemed beyond the resources of the people. The little girl wrote on her handkerchief a note: "This is all that I have," and wrapped it around fifty-seven cents. The story circulated all over the church—and outside it.

When the minister went to deal with the owners of

the lot, he confessed he did not have a down payment. But the man who owned the lot had been touched by the story of the girl's gift. "I will sell it to the church and take as down payment that fifty-seven cents you received. You can have as long as necessary to pay the rest."

Only God could have made the difference; that was not a valid business proposition. Because God touched the heart of a child, and the child touched the heart of an adult, Russell Conwell preached a sermon that swept the nation and raised millions of dollars for churches and humanitarian needs.

"But lay up for yourselves treasures in heaven . . ." Jesus said, "For where your treasure is, there will your heart be also" (Matthew 6:20, 21).

Before Southern Baptists set up the Cooperative Program, the first gift that was ever made to send a missionary to Africa came from a slave: fifteen dollars. The spark that touched off our missionary movement into that continent was the gift of this one woman; she had been admonished to do what she could, and she recognized God's dealings in her life. We never dared to realize the African continent would become the biggest mission field that Southern Baptists have.

What makes the difference? Following the principle stated by Jesus, "Where your treasure is, there will your heart be also."

Dr. Theron B. Rankin was secretary of our Foreign Mission Board. When he laid his father to rest, he went through his father's things and found an old checkbook. Checks were used sparingly fifty years ago, but there was a check for $6.80 that his father had made out to the Foreign Mission Board, an offering made before this son was born. Dr. Rankin hadn't known about that particular gift, but he had known how his father felt about missions. As a child growing up, his father's example concerning money had impressed his heart.

A little child didn't understand why his mother gave most of the flowers she grew to her neighbors. Being the errand boy, one day he complained about it when he came back. "Mother, why must you raise flowers and then give them away?"

"Son, smell your hands," his mother said.

He smelled his hands. "I still smell the flowers," he said wonderingly. The fragrance lingered on his hands.

You ought to put your stamp on life as it passes through your hands. In the impression that you leave, some kind of fragrance should linger.

What is real happiness? A London newspaper offered a large award for an essay on happiness. The first-place winner said: "Happiness is a craftsman whistling after a hard day's work. It is a child building castles in the sand. It is a mother bathing her newborn baby. It is a doctor smiling after difficult surgery. It is an honest man glad that honest toil is over." All of these things bring happiness because they are the accomplishments of a person's life.

One day you will understand what Jesus was saying. In the end, true happiness is not found in earthly values, but in eternal ones. One day you will go to collect your layaways, and I pray God that you will find treasure you have laid up in heaven.

10—KINGDOM:
The Divine Domain

Jesus said: *"Except a man be born again,
he cannot see the kingdom of God."*

John 3:3

The United States of America and its territories contain many different geographical boundaries. Sometimes we pass over the line from one state to another and scarcely notice.

If we should travel from the United States to another nation, however, we are made aware that we cross over a dividing line. The sun will set on both sides of that imaginary line at the same time, but it is definitely a jurisdictional boundary. When you return to the port of entry at that line, you have to prove in what nation you hold citizenship. Again and again many of us have proudly said, "I am a citizen of the United States of America."

But are you a citizen of the Kingdom of God? Whom do you worship? What is your pledge of allegiance? Have you crossed the definite line of commitment, of giving yourself over to God and saying, "I commit myself unto Him who is able to keep me from falling"? If you have, then you are a member of the Kingdom of God.

We may sing, "The Kingdom Is Coming," as if it is in

the future, but we are referring to something timeless. His Kingdom is past, present, and future.

The phrases *Kingdom of God* and *Kingdom of heaven* are used almost interchangeably in God's Word. But the local church and the Kingdom of God are not the same. It is possible to belong to the Kingdom and not belong to a church, because the moment you trust Jesus Christ as Saviour you become a child of God and a citizen of His Kingdom. You become a child of the Kingdom by your own choice. In the same manner, by another choice, you become a member of a local church.

The psalmist said, "Thy kingdom is an everlasting kingdom, and thy dominion endureth throughout all generations" (Psalms 145:13). Both heaven and earth are God's divine domain; His dominion is over all. The law of public domain is *the right of a government to take private property for public use by virtue of the superior dominion of sovereign power over all lands within its jurisdiction.*

All the world is under the jurisdiction of God. He holds absolute ownership, but He does not force anyone to salute His flag. He does not force any individual to accept citizenship without a voluntary commitment on the part of that individual. The sovereignty of God does not claim anyone against his will. However, each man or woman or child should commit himself to the dominion of God. In Matthew, we find that the Lord said, "But seek ye first the kingdom of God, and his righteousness; and all these things shall be added unto you" (Matthew 6:33).

Our country does not tax the church buildings in

which we worship. The state recognizes that they do not belong to the county, state, or city. They are the property of God's Kingdom. The rights to church buildings actually remain with and pass down to whomever comes after us as trustees. They belong to God.

People of many countries have immigrated to the United States and have become citizens of our nation voluntarily. They have gone before a magistrate and vowed, "I choose to become a citizen," and they take an oath of allegiance. In the same manner, we who are born children of this world, to become children of God, must make a commitment to God.

An earthly ruler can scarcely maintain rule over the bodies and outward actions of men. But God rules over the minds and spirits of men as well. We are not to confuse the inner and outer dominion.

Sometimes it is easier to say what the Kingdom of God is not than to understand what the Kingdom of God is. It must not be confused with the political kingdoms of this world, for they may be evil and they may do wrong. The Kingdom of God is never wrong. The children of the Kingdom may be wrong, but the Kingdom of God is the gracious, completely just, and glorious rule of God.

The Kingdom of God is not to be confused with the church. The church is only an agent of the Kingdom. The church age had a beginning; it is like a slot of time. The Kingdom of God is timeless. It had its beginning with God; it will have its consummation with the return of Jesus Christ to take charge on this earth. To become a citizen of the Kingdom of God requires that one accept Jesus Christ and obey His will.

This kingdom is mysterious in its conception, miraculous in its continuation, and matchless in its consummation.

Mysterious in Its Conception

Jesus made it very plain that His children are citizens of His Kingdom, a Kingdom that was *mysterious in its conception.* In the Bible, a mystery is not something for the curious, but a new and awesome revelation from God, something previously hidden which is revealed only at the proper time.

In 1862, Abraham Lincoln said to Congress, "Fellow citizens, we cannot escape history." In thinking of God's Kingdom, we cannot escape history, either. The patriarchs and the prophets are mentioned as part of the Kingdom: ". . . many shall come . . . and shall sit down with Abraham, and Isaac, and Jacob, in the kingdom of heaven" (Matthew 8:11).

Sometimes the Kingdom of God and the kingdom of Israel were spoken of almost as if they were one and the same, though certainly not all in the kingdom of Israel were necessarily citizens of the Kingdom of God. From the beginning of time, there have been believers in God. Any man who has reverently turned his mind and heart toward God and trusted Him with his life, within what was revealed to him by God, has become a citizen of God's Kingdom.

In the Old Testament we see many exhortations to and accounts of repentance. John the Baptist came preaching it as his single message: "In those days came John the Baptist, preaching . . . And saying, Repent ye: for the kingdom of heaven is at hand" (Matthew 3:1, 2). Someone has written, concerning that strange forerunner of Christ:

> Out of the desert he came,
> Out of the brooding rocks and sand,
>   Out of the flaming sun,
> John came striding,
> His eye on fire and his shaggy mane
>   A banner in the wind.

"The time is fulfilled," declared Jesus as He began His ministry, "and the kingdom of God is at hand: repent ye, and believe the gospel" (Mark 1:15). This is the same language that was used concerning physical birth in the Bible—the same word was used for a woman's time being *fulfilled*, when her child was born.

The Kingdom of God is ever present and growing among us or within us. We have national flags of our own design; we have pledges of allegiance men have written, but the territory of the Kingdom of God is within man.

Go yonder to Red China. Wherever there are those who have lifted up prayerful hearts to God and asked for His salvation, you can be sure that the Kingdom of God is among them.

Go to Soviet Russia. Wherever you find the people at worship, wherever they have lifted their hearts up to God, the Kingdom is among them.

Go to the most primitive parts of the jungle. Wherever people have lifted up their voices to God in prayerful repentance, then the Kingdom of God is among them.

The Kingdom is ageless and it is without boundaries. Wherever the cause of Christ has been accepted, where it has put down roots in one man's heart, then that heart has been claimed for the Kingdom of God. Wherever an explorer puts his flag, he claims land for his government. Jesus came out of heaven's glory, sent by the Father. When they erected that cross on Calvary's hill, Jesus planted the Kingdom of God among men.

When the dying thief turned to that One on the middle cross, he was not saying something he did not believe: "Lord, remember me when thou comest into thy kingdom" (Luke 23:42). Whatever the age of the individual and whatever his burden of sin, wherever someone has lifted up his heart and said, "Lord, remember me!" God has looked that way and the Kingdom of God has come in.

Jesus gave a new language for His Kingdom. In the fifth, sixth, and seventh chapters of Matthew we find prescriptions, recipes, definitions, if you please, of what the people of His Kingdom ought to be. The parables were also the language of His Kingdom. "It is characteristic of divine truth," said Ruskin, "that it should appear self-contradictory."

"Though I may not understand electricity," someone has said, "neither do I have to carry in my pocket a scientific textbook to be able to turn on a switch and enjoy the light."

The Jews hesitated to use the phrase, *Kingdom of God,* and in all of their teachings they used *kingdom of heaven,* instead. It was the custom of the Jewish teacher, in referring to God, to speak His name in a reverent and low tone. It was uttered almost in a whisper, from lip to ear. They endowed it with great reverence, so they used *kingdom of heaven* rather than *Kingdom of God.* But the two are one and the same. Jesus used *Kingdom of God,* and we claim the privilege to use it, also.

How is the Kingdom evidenced among us? Look at the parable of the soil in Matthew 13. Some seed fell on good ground and some fell on shallow ground and some fell on stony ground. Some men turned away and would not hear and did not receive the seed. But some did. Altogether, the Master Teacher gave at least ten parables concerning His Kingdom.

Miraculous in Its Continuation

The Kingdom of God is *miraculous in its continuation.* We may not have noticed the continuation of the Kingdom which is implied in the model prayer Jesus gave. We begin, "Thy kingdom come," and close with ". . . For thine is the kingdom, and the power, and the glory, for ever. Amen" (Matthew 6:10, 13).

The Kingdom began with the King. Jesus spoke its claim on Calvary. But the King and the Kingdom did not end on the cross, as some thought. The resurrection was proof of the power of the King and of the assured future of His eternal Kingdom.

In Luke 13:29 we read, "And they shall come from the east, and from the west, and from the north, and from the south, and shall sit down in the kingdom of God."

The world may go from church to church and check the parking lots and say that this Kingdom of God we talk about is a small thing—but it isn't!

God's Kingdom may not have marching bands, and God's soldiers may not parade with heavy artillery. We may not exhibit good-conduct ribbons such as are passed out by some governments. Maybe, in our human natures, we walk in broken step, but one day we shall stand before the Ruler of the universe and our Father will say, "Well done, good and faithful servant; thou hast been faithful over a few things, I will make thee ruler over many things: enter thou into the joy of thy lord" (Matthew 25:23).

The miracle of the Gospel of Jesus Christ is that the rule and reign of God continues in spite of opposition. The arithmetic of the Kingdom of God is not mere addition; rather, it is multiplication. It shall reach all the nations of the earth: "And this gospel of the kingdom shall be preached in all the world for a witness unto all nations . . ." (Matthew 24:14). You can be sure that God would not allow His church to die or the Kingdom to wither: ". . . and of his kingdom there shall be no end," said the angel to Mary (Luke 1:33).

Sometimes we feel that *we* are bringing in the Kingdom. We may have some place in the Kingdom of God—and I pray that we do—but Christ will bring in His Kingdom. The responsibility is in God's own hands. We have a King and we are His Kingdom. The only thing that is future is the uniting of the King and His Kingdom.

Matchless in Its Consummation

The Kingdom of God is *matchless in its consummation.* The King and Kingdom will one day be brought together.

In reply to those who wanted Him to use His heavenly power to establish an earthly kingdom, Jesus said, "My kingdom is not of this world." He was trying to tell His disciples that they were not the whole of the Kingdom of God, just a part of it. Here He wore no crown other than the crown of thorns that men gave Him. But He is, nevertheless, ruler of an everlasting kingdom.

On what premise is this Kingdom founded? To what do we owe its origins? What are its goals and objectives? As we analyze earthly kingdoms, we note their foundations. They have been founded on premises that range from ambition and dictatorship to democracy and religious principles.

But what are the premises for God's Kingdom? His is a spiritual Kingdom; its bounds are the bounds of the spirit. It is limitless and its realm is eternal. The foundation is God Himself and His love and righteousness.

It is claimed that George Frideric Handel wrote *The Messiah* in twenty-four days. Of the experience of writing that wonderful music, Handel said, "I did think I did see all of heaven before me, and the Great God Himself!"

It is impossible for us to take in all the grandeur of *The Messiah,* much less that of the Kingdom of God itself. We can catch a small glimpse as we read the words in Revelation: "The kingdoms of this world are become the kingdoms of our Lord, and of his Christ; and he shall reign for ever and ever" (Revelation 11:15).

How does one enter into such a Kingdom? To the scribe who recognized the validity of the greatest commandment Jesus gave, He said, "Thou art not far from the kingdom of God" (Mark 12:34). You may know of God's Kingdom; you may know the Christ of His Kingdom, but you are not a child of that Kingdom unless you have become His child by submission, obedience, and faith.

You must be willing to enter the Kingdom of God on His conditions, not yours. The Kingdom is found by those who seek it diligently. Jesus illustrated this with the parables of the lost treasure and the pearl of great price. But God's treasures are out of the reach of those who will not open their hearts to Him. Faith and humility are steps on the threshold to the Kingdom.

"Except ye be converted, and become as little children," Jesus said, "ye shall not enter into the kingdom of heaven. Whosoever therefore shall humble himself as this little child, the same is greatest in the kingdom of heaven" (Matthew 18:3, 4).

Another characteristic of a small child is that he is willing to forgive others and he is greatly hurt if he is not forgiven by others. We must be willing to forgive and desire to be forgiven.

Christ's command was "seek ye *first* the kingdom of God." One of the great scholars has said that our English word *seek* is not strong enough to translate this concept. In the original language, it actually means "to storm the gates." How much do you want to be a part of God's Kingdom? Any price that has to be paid, any sacrifice that you must make, anything you must give up, is worth it to become a child of the Kingdom of God.

Has God's will been done on earth in your heart? The final entrance requirement of God's Kingdom is submission. The Lord taught us to pray, "Thy kingdom come, thy will be done." There can be no Kingdom where there is no King, and there is no King unless there are faithful subjects.

If you have not accepted Christ, you are not a citizen of the Kingdom of God and you cannot claim God as Father. Of whose kingdom are you a citizen? The day you say "I will" to God, you enter in.

The Kingdom of God begins in the heart and is consummated in the presence of God. There is never any defeat, any decay, any end to it. In God's domain, He does not draft you. You must be willing to say on bended knee, with bowed head and committed life, "I belong to Christ; I give myself to Him."